The Incompetent Teacher

Hoagland

The Incompetent Teacher:

Managerial Responses

Edwin M. Bridges

A Revised and Extended Edition

The contents of this book were developed under a grant from the National Institute of Education, US Department of Education. However, these contents do not necessarily represent the policy of the Department of Education, and you should not assume endorsement by the Federal Government.

The names of the teachers and administrators which appear in this book have been changed to protect their right to privacy.

The Falmer Press

(A member of the Taylor & Francis Group)
Washington, D.C. • London

| USA | The Falmer Press, Taylor & Francis Inc., 1900 Frost Road, Suite 101, Bristol, PA 19007 |
| UK | The Falmer Press, 4 John Street, London WC1N 2ET |

First published 1986
Reprinted 1989
Revised and extended edition 1992
Reprinted 1993

Library of Congress Cataloging in Publication Data

Bridges, Edwin M.
    The incompetent teacher.

    Bibliography: p.
    Includes index.
    1. Teachers—United States—Rating of. 2. School supervision—United States. I. Title.
    LB2838.B685 1986 371.1'44 85-27588
    ISBN 1-85000-087-5
    ISBN 0-75070-050-5 (pbk.)

Jacket design by Caroline Archer

Typeset in 11/13 Bembo by
Graphicraft Typesetters Ltd., Hong Kong

Printed in Great Britain by Burgess Science Press, Basingstoke on paper which has a specified pH value on final paper manufacture of not less than 7.5 and is therefore 'acid free'.

Contents

To my wife Marjorie
and my four children
Bruce, Brian, Rebecca and Rick.

Preface

When the first edition of *The Incompetent Teacher* appeared, I privately harbored some doubts about my claim that the administrative responses to teacher incompetence which I uncovered in California prevail elsewhere. Subsequent experiences have erased most, if not all, of these doubts.

Shortly after the publication of this book, I was invited to the People's Republic of China to lecture on the subject of teacher incompetence. Chinese officials view teacher incompetence as a serious problem and estimate that there are three million such teachers in their country. These officials were eager to hear about how American administrators dealt with this problem. Midway through my three-hour lecture on this topic (fortified by aspirins for a fever, Chinese medication for stomach cramps, and pills laced with opium for diarrhea), we recessed for 15 minutes. Dozens of Chinese rushed to the front of the lecture hall and animatedly conversed with my interpreter. When they left, he looked at me and said, 'They were astonished to learn that the Americans deal with incompetent teachers the same way they [the Chinese] do'. He went on to say that Chinese administrators, like their American counterparts, are hampered in dealing with the problem by teacher tenure (referred to in their country as 'the iron rice bowl'). Several weeks later I visited Hong Kong. A professor at the Chinese University of Hong Kong had read my book and invited me and my wife to dinner. During our dinner conversation, he said, 'I am a former headmaster of a school in Hong Kong; it's like you wrote your book about what's happening here'.

Reviews of the book elsewhere paint a similar picture. In England, Canada, and Australia reviewers noted that the research was conducted primarily in California; however, the results were applicable to their own country. One reviewer, a former administrator on the east coast of the United States, offered an opinion that is reflective of the reactions which have been expressed throughout various regions of the world:

> *The Incompetent Teacher* is the outcome of three research studies on how administrators in California deal with incompetent teachers. The data drawn from the studies, in addition to a survey of the literature on teacher incompetence, leads the author to conclude that the behaviors of California school administrators are not idiosyncratic, and that it is likely administrators respond similarly in the rest of the country. While evidence for this generalization is admittedly limited, most readers will judge Bridges' presumption accurate on the basis of personal experience. (*The Principals' Center Newsletter*, Harvard Graduate School of Education)

As part of this same review, the author also commented,

> There is the gratification of finding research evidence to substantiate what our personal experience has shown us to be so. As Bridges' tale of largely standardized, yet unsuccessful, personnel practices unfolds, it is difficult not to nod one's head in recognition.

Taken together, these fragments of evidence strengthen my confidence in the portrait that I have painted based on my studies in California. The responses of administrators to teacher incompetence which I unearthed in the Golden State apparently cover a much larger part of the globe than I ever dreamed possible.

In preparing the revision to this original work, I have chosen to add two new chapters and to leave the rest intact. One of the new chapters describes a relatively rare response of administrators to the problem of incompetence — dismissal. The other new chapter discusses how my own thinking about the problem of teacher quality has changed since the initial publication of my book. I propose a number of radical changes in teaching policy, including one that raises the standard of performance expected for teachers who have tenure.

Before going to press with the second edition of the book, I considered changing its title and cover (featuring three green apples, one blemished). The original title and cover generated strong reactions, usually negative. The reactions have been so intense that I felt at times like someone who has been charged with blasphemy. After spending five years studying and thinking about a controversial subject, it is distressing to learn that some people are so outraged by the book's cover that they refuse to read what I have learned about the problem and how administrators are dealing with it. Despite these unwelcome reactions, I have decided to stay with the original title in hopes that most readers will react as one reviewer did:

> I wish that the title and cover of the book (featuring a blemished green apple) gave a less negative impression. I found this a minor barrier to getting started on reading *The Incompetent Teacher*. Once this barrier was overcome the book became increasingly absorbing. (*Curriculum Perspectives*)

A work of this magnitude is never a solo operation, and I would like to express appreciation to those who have contributed their time, thoughts, and data to this undertaking. Approximately two hundred administrators shared their insights and their practices with me. Without their wholehearted cooperation, I never could have acquired an understanding of how administrators are dealing with the problem of teacher incompetence. Although the reactions of teachers to this problem are reflected more in the revision than in the first version of the book, their views on this important issue remain underrepresented. I hope that other researchers will be stimulated by my work to examine this sensitive and controversial issue through the eyes of classroom teachers.

Three individuals have played an especially crucial role in this endeavor. My research assistant, Barry Groves, was invaluable in helping me to collect the data from administrators. He conducted half of the interviews and gathered the information for the case study. The dexterity of my daughter, Rebecca, on the computer made it possible for me to meet my writing deadlines. She also let me know when I was unclear and talking too much like a professor.

The third individual who played a key role in the preparation of this book is Henry M. Levin. From the first day I expressed interest in the problem of teacher incompetence, he has been a steady source of encouragement and an influential force in securing funding for this project. His pre-publication reviews of the manuscript were filled with insightful and valuable suggestions. If not for him, I never would have experienced the joy that occurs when work is play.

Chapter 1

Introduction

The Problem

Our story opens in the classroom of a teacher who typifies the problem that is being addressed in this book.

> Mrs. Kilpatrick, a third grade teacher who acquired tenure in 1967, is seated at her desk. Several students come to her with questions about the homework assignment. Each one is told the same thing, 'Go back and think about it'. Mrs. Kilpatrick notices two children talking in the back of the room and throws an eraser at them. Shortly thereafter, she gets up from her desk and approaches a child who is obviously having trouble doing the assignment. She taps the child on the head with her fingernails and says in a belittling tone of voice, 'Are you so dumb that you can't do that?'
>
> Across the room are several bright students who have finished their work. They sit with bored looks on their faces.
>
> Down the hall Mrs. Kilpatrick's latest Principal stares at several documents lying on his desk. Eight parents have requested that their children be transferred out of her class. The reading specialist has filed a written report about Mrs. Kilpatrick's reading program. Half of the students are misplaced; they are reading texts covered the previous year. Formal reading instruction is non-existent. Mrs. Kilpatrick merely has students read aloud in 'round robin' fashion, and she never makes a comment. In the opinion of the reading specialist and the eight parents, Mrs. Kilpatrick is an incompetent teacher. Somewhat reluctantly, the Principal has reached the same conclusion.[1]

Although incompetent teachers, like Mrs. Kilpatrick, represent a relatively small proportion of the teaching force in the United States, the number of students who are being taught by such teachers is substantial. If we assume that 5 per cent of the teachers in public elementary and secondary schools are incompetent (Johnson, 1984; Neill and Custis, 1978),[2] the number of students who are being taught by these teachers exceeds the total combined public school enrollments of fourteen states: Alaska, Delaware, Hawaii, Idaho, Maine, Montana, Nebraska, Nevada, New Hampshire, North Dakota, Rhode Island, South Dakota, Vermont and Wyoming.[3] The large number of students who are being shortchanged each year by incompetent teachers underscores the importance and the seriousness of this problem.[4]

Not surprisingly, parents are unhappy about the presence of such teachers in the teaching profession. For twenty consecutive years, parents have expressed their reservations about teaching quality in annual polls of the public's attitudes toward the public schools. On one occasion nearly half of the public school parents indicated that there were teachers in the local schools who should be fired. The most frequently cited reason for this drastic action was incompetence (Elam, 1978). Recently, parents in districts with declining enrollments have begun to question layoff policies which ignore the problem of teacher incompetence. The following letter illustrates the intense feelings which some parents have about layoffs based on seniority rather than on performance:

Who says newspapers don't print good news? I've just read in my morning paper that the Principal and a group of parents at Johnson Junior High School are going to try to do something about the current system of deciding which teachers get laid off.

Over the years, as a parent, I repeatedly felt frustrated, angry and helpless when each spring teachers — who were the ones the students hoped anxiously to get, who had students visiting their classrooms after school, who had lively looking classrooms — would receive their lay-off notices. Meanwhile, left behind to teach our children, would be the mediocre teachers who appeared to have precious little creative inspiration for teaching and very little interest in children.

I do not mean to paint all teachers with the same brush. There are many excellent teachers in the Union School District, and in all the districts. But we had to work to find them. In our case it required changing schools. Not all parents have the time and energy to take this drastic step. And why should they have to? And, at the high school level, even this choice is closed off.

My son, now in high school, was fortunate enough to have had Andrew Morganstein as a teacher. When he read the article he said, 'Oh no, they can't fire Mr. Morganstein'.

Oh yes, son. They can and they did. But my sons are used to the yearly spring disaster. They have seen it happen year after year.

One wonders what the young people think of this system. Does it make them wonder if excellence is worthwhile, or is it enough to be just mediocre?

Students and parents are not the only ones who are being shortchanged by incompetent teachers. These poor performers tarnish the vast majority of America's teachers who are competent and conscientious professionals. Witness a 1984 issue of *Newsweek* magazine. The cover pictures a teacher wearing a dunce cap and carries the headline, 'Why Teachers Fail'. The accompanying article paints a dismal portrait of the teaching profession — low SAT scores, easy admission requirements, and intellectually sterile training. Questionable competence is the underlying message, and the authors (Williams *et al.*, 1984) make no effort to mute it. Articles like this suggest that incompetence is either more pervasive or more serious in the teaching profession than elsewhere in our society. The suggestion casts a dark shadow on the thousands of competent teachers who are overworked, underpaid and underappreciated for their efforts and accomplishments.

Quite understandably, the problem of teacher incompetence has not gone unnoticed by educational reformers. They have advanced numerous solutions such as: (i) cleanse the profession by removing the incompetent teachers; (ii) improve the attractiveness of the teaching profession by raising salaries; (iii) restrict entry into the profession by means of competency tests; (iv) upgrade the quality of preservice teacher education by adopting competency-based preparation programs; and (v) provide incentives for quality teaching by instituting merit pay.

Although there appears to be no shortage of ideas about what should be done to redress the problem of teacher incompetence, there is virtually nothing known about the ways in which local school officials are actually dealing with this important problem. This book represents an initial exploration of this hitherto uncharted area and seeks to illuminate the following questions:

1   What is the nature of teacher incompetence?
2   How do administrators ascertain who the incompetent teachers are?
3   What are the perceived causes of teacher incompetence?
4   What are the various ways in which school administrators respond to the problem of teacher incompetence?
5   What are the factors which shape their responses?

In the remainder of this chapter we discuss what we have learned about the first three questions and foreshadow the major topics to be addressed in subsequent chapters. It will become evident that the bulk of this book is devoted to a fine-grained description of how administrators respond to the problem of teacher incompetence and a comprehensive analysis of the conditions which shape these responses.

The Nature of Incompetence

Incompetence is a concept without precise technical meaning (Rosenberger and Plimpton, 1975).[5] Although most state legislatures have singled out incompetence (or one of its blood relatives — inefficiency, gross inefficiency, and inadequate performance) as a legal cause for dismissing teachers, only two states, Alaska and Tennessee, have attempted to define the term. Neither state supplies any criteria or standards for determining what constitutes incompetent performance in the classroom.

In the absence of state legislation, the courts have shown little inclination to specify the criteria and the standards by which incompetence can be evaluated. One notable exception to this trend is the Michigan Court of Appeals which ruled in 1979 that

> School boards and the Tenure Commission should, in each case, make specific determinations concerning the challenged teacher's *knowledge of his subject*, his *ability to impart it*, the *manner and efficacy of his discipline* over his students, his *rapport with parents and other teachers*, and his *physical and mental ability to withstand the strain of teaching*. In each case, the effect on the school and its students of the acts alleged to require dismissal must be delineated.[6]

The Michigan Tenure Commission subsequently adopted these criteria as its definition of incompetency but held that all five factors need not be established to support a charge of incompetence. Any one of these factors is sufficient.[7] It should be noted, however, that neither the Michigan Court of Appeals nor the Tenure Commission established any clear-cut standards for judging whether a teacher has satisfied these criteria.

Lacking firm guidance from state statutes and the courts, administrators are generally left on their own to figure out what the criteria, standards or both should be for determining whether a teacher is incompetent. As we argue in the next chapter, the absence of definite standards or unequivocal cut-off points is especially troublesome for administrators in California and elsewhere because the burden of proof rests on them to demonstrate that a teacher is incompetent. Successful dismissal of a tenured teacher for incompetence hinges upon the administrator's ability to persuade an impartial third-party that (s)he has provided such proof.

Our research sheds some light on how administrators cope with the definitional uncertainty inherent in using incompetence as a reason for weeding teachers out of local school districts. Incompetence, as reflected in the personnel decisions of the administrators whom we studied, appears to mean persistent failure in one or more of the following respects:

1   failure to maintain discipline;
2   failure to treat students properly;
3   failure to impart subject matter effectively;
4   failure to accept teaching advice from superiors;
5   failure to demonstrate mastery of the subject matter being taught; and
6   failure to produce the intended or desired results in the classroom.

The most common type of failure is weakness in maintaining discipline. This particular form of failure is the leading cause for dismissal in studies of teacher failure which have been conducted over the past seventy years (Littler, 1914; Buellesfield, 1915; Madsen, 1927; Simon, 1936; Bridges and Gumport, 1984).

Incompetency ordinarily manifests itself in a pattern of recurring instances, rather than in a single egregious incident (Tigges, 1965; Rosenberger and Plimpton, 1975). Because there are no clear-cut standards or yardsticks for determining whether a teacher has failed to meet a particular criterion, supervisors must accumulate numerous examples of a teacher's shortcomings to demonstrate that a pattern of failure exists. The significance of a demonstrable pattern of deficiencies is underscored in the following court ruling:

> Proof of momentary lapses in discipline or of a single day's lesson gone awry is not sufficient to show cause for dismissal of a tenured teacher... Yet, where brief instances and isolated lapses occur repeatedly, there emerges a pattern of behavior which, if deficient, will support the dismissal of a tenured teacher. Where the school board fails ... to show that the examples of conduct constitute a pattern of deficiency, then dismissal cannot be permitted.[8]

When administrators seek to remove a teacher for incompetence, the teacher is often in a state of 'performance collapse'. The teacher's performance is so bad that no one doubts the appropriateness of the label, 'incompetent'. The scope of the incompetent teacher's failure is illustrated by the following description of a teacher who resigned under pressure rather than face dismissal:

> Mrs. Ingalls is in her early sixties and has taught at the elementary level in the district for more than twenty years. During this time, she has taught in six different schools. Each time she came under fire she transferred to another school within the' district. The students in Mrs. Ingalls' class are making little or no academic progress. Six parents have requested that their children not be assigned to Mrs. Ingalls next year. It is common knowledge that she has no control over her class and frequently refers trouble-makers to the Principal. She also lacks self-control and abuses kids when she becomes angry. Students complain about being called stupid and about being slapped, grabbed, and pinched. When she isn't yelling at students, they still don't pay attention because her classroom teaching reflects inadequate lesson planning. Her behavior is offensive to other teachers, as well as parents, students, and administrators.

The standards which are used to judge a teacher's competence appear to vary from one district to another. Although incompetent teachers are often viewed as the dregs of a district's teaching force, they may on occasion be average or just slightly below average in relation to teachers in other districts. In the absence of clear-cut standards for judging the competency of a teacher, comparative judgments inevitably creep into the evaluation process. Sometimes these comparisons work to the detriment of teachers who are poor only in comparison with other teachers in their school or district. As one principal put it,

> She (a teacher in the primary grades) looked weak in comparison with the other teachers on my staff who were outstanding. We hired a specialist in classroom management to work with her for a few days. He felt that she was better than a lot of teachers he had worked with who had been judged to be marginal or okay in other districts. In my school, okay isn't good enough. My parents insist on the best.

Given the ambiguity surrounding the meaning of incompetence, it is understandable how comparative judgments can color its perception and definition in any particular setting.

The Detection of Incompetence

School officials cast a broad net to identify the poor performers in the classroom. Recognizing that most of a teacher's activities take place behind closed doors, administrators use a variety of means to detect the incompetent teacher: supervisor ratings; student, parent, and teacher complaints; student surveys; and student test results (see table 1). In view of the limitations and questionable soundness of some of these methods, the reliance on multiple sources represents a reasonable decision.

Most districts (72.3 per cent) use at least three different methods to identify incompetent teachers. The most frequently reported methods are (i) supervisor ratings and observations; (ii) complaints from parents or students; (iii) complaints from other teachers; and (iv) student test

Table 1: Practices Used by California School Districts to Identify Incompetent Teachers

Practice	Per cent of districts (n = 141) reporting use
Supervisor observations/ratings	100.0
Complaints from parents or students	78.0
Complaints from other teachers	53.2
Student test results	46.0
Follow-up surveys of former students	26.9
Student ratings	15.6
Exit interviews with parents	4.3
Other (number of Ds and Fs given; number of student referrals for discipline problems; attendance of teacher)	2.1

results. The decision to rely on more than supervisory ratings is important for several reasons. First, supervisors, especially principals, do not allocate a significant portion of their time to managing instructional activities (Hallinger, 1983). In place of coordinating and controlling the curriculum and instructional program of the school, principals spend most of their workday on managerial tasks that are unrelated to these matters (Peterson, 1977–78; Sproull, 1981).

Second, even when supervisors observe a teacher in the classroom, they may not see a representative sample of the teacher's performance. If the Principal is required by the union contract to announce classroom observations in advance or chooses to do so as a professional courtesy, (s)he may be watching a staged, polished presentation that is atypical of the teacher's behavior. By way of illustration, one Personnel Director gave the following account:

> This teacher (Miss Noll) was a real faker. For two years she received flawless, glowing evaluations. She was able to do a perfect lesson in front of the Special Services Coordinator and the Principal, but she slacked off when they were not there. They had no idea that the teacher was doing nothing in the classroom. She fooled her previous supervisors, too. She had absolutely glowing letters of recommendation from four different administrators.

Third, supervisory ratings are questionable indicators of how much students are learning.[9] Most of the research which bears on this issue shows no relationship between supervisory ratings and student performance on achievement tests; representative conclusions drawn from these studies are as follows:

> ... superintendents, supervisors, and principals tended to rate good teachers low and poor teachers high (goodness defined by pupil growth in achievement).... Ratings by superintendents, supervisors, principals should not be accepted as the sole or valid criteria until persons in these positions have been re-educated for this responsibility (McCall and Krause, 1959).

> ... evaluations based on ... supervisors' ratings and those based on measures of pupil growth and achievement were not significantly correlated (Anderson, 1954).

> Whatever pupil gain measures in relation to teaching ability it is not that emphasized in supervisory ratings (Jones, 1946).

Employer's ratings of teaching ability are not related to pupil gains in information (Brookover, 1940).

In the one study that reports a positive, but modest, relationship between supervisory ratings and student achievement, the author (Murnane, 1984) concludes, 'If terms of employment were a function of assessed performance, the terms offered to any individual teacher would be very sensitive to the choice of instrument (ratings or tests of student achievement) used to measure performance'. It should be noted that the questionable soundness of supervisory ratings[10] is not limited to the field of education. Research on the trustworthiness of supervisory ratings in business and industry indicates that they are frequently loaded with subjectivity and bias and are neither as reliable nor as valid as peer ratings (Latham and Wexley, 1981).

To overcome the problems inherent in using supervisory ratings, administrators also use complaints from students and parents to identify ineffective teachers. Complaints signal that something may be radically wrong in a teacher's classroom and stimulate a closer look at what is happening. They also represent a source of pressure on the administrator to deal with the poor performer. The crucial significance of these complaints will become evident when we later examine their role in overcoming the reluctance of administrators to confront incompetent teachers.

Complaints from teachers also figure in the identification of unsatisfactory teachers. These complaints arise in large part because of the interdependent character of teaching activities (Johnson, 1984). The incompetent teacher creates several potential problems for his or her colleagues. Most of the poor performers are unable to maintain discipline; if students become too unruly, the noise may disrupt the instruction taking place in other classrooms. The students who have been taught by these teachers also may create difficulties for subsequent teachers if the students have not mastered the concepts, skills, and material to which they have been exposed. Finally, incompetent teachers may become a source of frustration for their colleagues if they work together as members of a teaching team. Any one of these problems may prompt other teachers to complain. The 'faker' who was mentioned earlier provides a vivid illustration of the role teacher complaints can play in identifying incompetent teachers. According to the Personnel Director,

Miss Noll was a shirker. She frequently left class and talked on the phone for long periods. She often returned late from lunch.

She didn't follow the curriculum either; no math had been taught in her class for thirteen weeks. She didn't prepare lesson plans and ridiculed students when they didn't pay attention. *The supervisors had no inkling of this until the co-teacher and instructional aides came forward to complain.* Up to that time, the supervisors thought that she was an ideal teacher. What this teacher really was was an ideal faker.

In addition to supervisory ratings and complaints from students, parents, and other teachers, school district officials monitor student test results and use these to identify the poorly performing teachers. Using these tests to evaluate the effectiveness of teachers is not without its problems, however. The effects of teachers on the achievement of different groups of students are relatively unstable or inconsistent from one year to the next (Rosenshine, 1977). Moreover, these effects are even unstable from one topic to another for the *same* students (*Ibid*). Even if the effects were stable, the tests may not measure knowledge and skills which match the instructional objectives of the district or the teacher. Finally, the performance of a teacher's students on these tests may be attributable in part to initial differences in the performance potential of the students.

The least frequently used ways of identifying the incompetent teacher, in descending order of usage, are follow-up surveys of former students, student ratings,[11] and exit interviews with parents. Districts also report using such indicators as the number of Ds and Fs given by a teacher, the number of student referrals for disciplinary reasons, and the attendance record of the teacher. However, these last three indicators are rarely used.

The Roots of Incompetence

When teachers are having difficulties in their classrooms, their unsatisfactory performance may stem from one or more of the following causes: (i) shortcomings of the supervisor and/or organization; (ii) shortcomings of the employee; and (iii) outside or non-job-related influences affecting the employee (Steinmetz, 1969). The causes of the incompetent teacher's difficulties appear to be multi-faceted. Administrators attribute the poor performance of such teachers to both external and internal causes. One external cause for the teacher's problems is inadequate supervision. Some supervisors lack the skills to deal effectively with incompetent teachers and fail to take corrective action early in the teacher's career when this guidance may be beneficial.

In the vast majority of cases administrators attributed the causes of the teacher's poor performance to two or more sources. The most commonly perceived cause was shortcomings of the teacher, and the most prevalent shortcoming was the teacher's lack of ability or skill in performing instructional duties. For the most part, administrators did not elaborate on what they meant by ability or skill deficiencies. In those instances where administrators did specify the nature of the deficiencies, they tended to emphasize weak intellectual ability, inadequate knowledge of the subject, and poor judgment. By way of illustration, administrators made comments like the following:

> She was dumb as a stone.

> She wasn't very bright.

> She wasn't on top of the subject matter.

> She lacked common sense.

Administrators also attributed the incompetent teacher's difficulties to lack of effort. They described the motivational states of these teachers in the following ways:

> She was not putting forth the effort. She met her classes but minimally met her teaching obligations.

> He was lazy, not interested in teaching.

> She wasn't highly motivated, just putting in time.

> He didn't have any desire to improve and kept repeating the same stupid mistakes. Discipline problems didn't seem to bother him. He was really laid back, low key.

Lack of effort was less prevalent than ability or skill as a perceived cause of the teacher's problems in the classroom.[12] In a few cases, administrators even portrayed the poor performers as 'trying hard but simply not getting any results'.

Insufficient ability and motivation were not the only individual shortcomings which administrators perceived to be at the root of a teacher's difficulties. In nearly half of the cases, teachers suffered from some type of personal disorder or pathology that adversely affected their performance. Emotional distress, burn-out, and health problems were relatively common. Alcoholism was mentioned only twice as a major source of the teacher's difficulties.

Besides the personal inadequacies of teachers, administrators also attributed unsatisfactory performance to outside influences.[13] Marital difficulties and financial problems were commonplace. Several of the teachers had gone through arduous divorces while other teachers were distracted by the continual turmoil in their marriages. In some of the cases, it is clear from the comments of administrators that these outside influences preceded the teacher's difficulties in the classroom. In other cases the data fail to reveal whether the teacher's problems, particularly marital problems, preceded or coincided with the difficulties being experienced at work. These teachers may have been caught in some vicious cycle in which the problems at home and work fed on one another and created a downward spiral in both settings.

Finally, administrators assigned partial blame for the teacher's present difficulties to the shortcomings of past supervisors. According to some of our interviewees, these supervisors lacked the ability to deal with incompetent teachers and were reluctant to confront them about their poor performance in the classroom. One administrator bluntly stated, 'He had incompetent supervisors who didn't help him to improve'. Another administrator blamed the teacher's current problems on supervisory passivity; in the words of this administrator,

> Her supervisors were aware of the problems but did nothing. If they had confronted her and given her assistance, she might have been salvaged and transformed into an adequate teacher.

A third administrator implicated the competence and the motivation of 'previous principals who lacked the skill and the willingness to give poor evaluations'. These three administrators were not isolated examples; there were several other administrators who explicitly held supervisors partially responsible for the troubles being experienced by incompetent teachers.

By way of concluding this discussion of the roots of incompetence, we wish to underscore how complex the origins appear to be. Rarely, is a teacher's poor performance due solely to a single cause like effort, skill or ability. More commonly, unsatisfactory performance stems from other sources as well, such as personal disorders, marital problems, and inadequate supervision. Under these conditions, efforts to improve the performance of such teachers represent a formidable challenge and undertaking. It is unlikely that something akin to a miracle drug or an organ transplant will ever suffice as a cure for the problem of incompetent teaching. The extent of the teacher's difficulties in the classroom and the causes which underlie these difficulties are simply too far-reaching.

The Responses

A major portion of this book, as noted earlier, is devoted to a fine-grained description of the ways in which school administrators respond to incompetent teachers. The discussion of these responses is interlaced with comments from the administrators who were interviewed and with excerpts from documents taken from the personnel files of incompetent teachers. Readers will have the opportunity to step behind the closed doors of local school districts and to inspect first-hand the contents of documents like the following: the classroom observation reports of principals, the annual evaluations of incompetent teachers, the formal notices of incompetency, and the written reactions of teachers to what is being said about them. We show how the contents of these documents reflect four different types of administrative responses to incompetent teachers: (i) tolerance of the teacher's poor performance; (ii) an attempt to salvage the incompetent teacher; (iii) an effort to induce the poor performer to resign or to retire early; and (iv) a recommendation for dismissal.

Tolerance of the Poor Performer

Our research has uncovered several ways in which administrators exhibit a reluctance to confront the incompetent teacher. These various responses to the poor performer are discussed in chapter 2 and are contrasted with the responses which have been observed in the Fortune 500 companies and in other professions. One response, the use of escape hatches to sidestep the problems by the incompetent teacher, is especially interesting. The reader will learn what these escape hatches are and how they are used. These escape hatches simultaneously protect the incompetent teacher and minimize the destructive consequences of his/her ineptitude on the organization.

Salvage Attempts

Once administrators decide to confront an incompetent teacher about his/her poor performance, they usually focus their efforts on how to improve the teacher's effectiveness in the classroom. In chapter 3 we identify the salient features of these salvage attempts. The discussion discloses the ¦limited success of these rescue operations and explains why they rarely result in dramatic improvement. Those who maintain that remediation is the way to solve the problem of teacher incompetence will not discover much support for their view in this book. If the teacher is a veteran with many years of experience, the problem is indeed formidable and, perhaps, untreatable. Conceivably, remediation is effective, but only at the early stages of a person's teaching career when his/her teaching style is still malleable.

Induced Exits

When, and if, the salvage attempt fails, administrators begin to concentrate their efforts on how to get rid of the incompetent teacher. If the teacher has tenure, as most do, administrators try to induce a resignation or an early retirement. In chapter 4 we discuss the dynamics of these induced exits and analyze the role of pressure, negotiations, teacher unions, and inducements (what the teacher requests and/or receives in return for his/her resignation) in these induced departures. Pressure is especially influential in securing the resignations of incompetent teachers. We show why this is the case and describe the kinds of pressure which administrators exert on these teachers.

The role played by teacher unions in the induced resignations of incompetent teachers is of special interest. The popular view is that these unions are chiefly responsible for the continued employment of ineffective teachers (Johnson, 1984). Our research provides an opportunity to assess the validity of this view by examining how teacher unions behave when administrators attempt to induce the incompetents to resign. Are teacher unions staunch defenders of the incompetent teacher? Are they passive by-standers? Or, are they silent allies of the administration? The answer lies in chapters 4 and 6.

Dismissals

The Determinants

In the next chapter, we discuss a variety of personal and situational factors which influence the inclinations of administrators to tolerate or to confront incompetent teachers. Teacher tenure and the administrator's desire to avoid conflict promote tolerant and protective responses while parental complaints and declining enrollments exert pressure on the administrator to confront the poor performer. Whether the administrator actually confronts the teacher in the face of these pressures depends in part on the size of the district and the financial health of the district. Small is beautiful when it comes to confronting the poor performer, and budget slashing has stimulated administrators to weed out the deadwood. Our analysis reveals why.

Summary

This book focuses on how school administrators deal with the problem of teacher incompetence. Although incompetent teachers may constitute only 5 per cent of the teaching force, they tarnish the reputation of the entire profession, shortchange nearly two million students a year, and engender parental dissatisfaction with the public schools. Despite the importance of this problem, little is known about how local school administrators are handling the substandard teachers on their staffs. To understand what is happening, we conducted several studies in California, a state that accounts for almost one-tenth of the students and teachers in the United States, and reviewed the research on practices and conditions in other states. These various sources of information provide an in-depth understanding of how administrators respond to the incompetent teacher and the conditions which shape these responses. Our research also throws limited light on the nature of teacher incompetence, the ways in which administrators detect it, and the causal factors which account for the teacher's difficulties in the classroom.

We began our analysis of the problem by discussing the nature of teacher incompetence, the ways in which administrators detect it, and the underlying causes of incompetence in the classroom. Incompetence is a concept without precise technical meaning; the lack of clear-cut standards for judging teacher incompetence results in variable standards being used across school districts. Within each district the incompetent teachers are the worst of the lot; no one doubts that they are incompetent because most are in a state of 'performance collapse'. The vast majority of school districts use at least three different means to identify incompetent teachers; the most frequently reported methods are supervisory observations, complaints from parents or students, complaints from other teachers, and student test results. Given the limitations of each indicator, the reliance on multiple measures appears to represent a sound practice. The difficulties which incompetent teachers experience in the classroom often stem from multiple causes: the personal short-comings of the teacher, non-job-related influences (for example, marital and financial difficulties), and the limitations or failings of supervisors. The multi-faceted character of these underlying causes poses a real challenge for those intent on treating the problem of incompetent teaching.

We concluded this chapter by foreshadowing the topics to be addressed in subsequent chapters. The description and analysis will center on four kinds of responses to the poor performer (namely, tolerant and protective actions, rescue attempts, induced resignations and dismissals) and the situational conditions which affect how administrators actually respond. Teacher tenure is one of these conditions. It hampers to some extent the ability of school districts to maintain a high quality teaching staff because once a teacher acquires tenure, blatant failure, not competence, becomes the standard for judging whether a teacher is entitled to remain in the classroom. In the last two chapters we explore what the implications of this shift in standards are for policies and practices in the area of teacher evaluation.

Notes

1 This teacher was charged with incompetence and unprofessional conduct; the information was taken from the report of the Commission on Professional Competence. This three-member Commission conducts dismissal hearings in California and decides whether a school district has substantiated its charges against the teacher. The other portraits of incompetent teachers which appear in this book are drawn from the case histories of incompetent teachers who were induced to resign or take early retirement. See Appendix A for details about these case histories.
2 The estimates range from 5 to 15 per cent. Since the estimates are based on inexact measures of incompetence, we have chosen to use the lower estimate. We fully acknowledge that this estimate may overstate or understate the true incidence of incompetence in the teaching profession. As a result, we have purposely chosen the phrase, 'if we *assume*', to introduce our discussion of the numerical prevalence of incompetence in the teaching force.
3 The number of students was estimated as follows. In the fall of 1981 there were 2,124,697 full-time equivalent teachers employed in the United States (Grant and Snyder, 1984). Five per cent of this figure is 106,235, the estimated number of incompetent teachers. We assumed that each of these teachers taught 18.9 students (the average pupil-teacher ratio reported for 1981–82). Under this assumption, the total number of students being

taught by incompetent teachers is 2,007,842. This number exceeds the total combined public school enrollments reported in 1981–82 for the fourteen smallest states.

4 The problem of teacher incompetence is not limited to the United States. All of the English headteachers interviewed by Grace (1984) acknowledged the existence of poor or incompetent teachers.

5 Definitions of teacher incompetence can be found in Kelleher (1985), Rosenberger and Plimpton (1975), Tigges (1965), and Harper and Gammon (1981).

6 Beebe v. Haslett Pub. Sch., 66 Mich. App., 718 at 726 (1970).

7 Niemi v. Board of Education, Kearsley Sch. Dist., TTC 74–36.

8 Board of Education v. Ingels, 394 N.E. 2d 69 (1979).

9 Few studies have focused on the effectiveness of supervisory ratings in promoting teacher improvement. In fact, we were able to locate only one study that investigated this important issue. Tuckman and Oliver (1968) designed an experiment to test the relative effects of feedback on teacher's behavior. There were four feedback conditions in this study: (i) students only; (ii) supervisor (either the Principal, Vice-Principal, or Assistant Principal); (iii) students and supervisors; and (iv) no feedback. The researchers found that teachers react to feedback, irrespective of source; however, the reaction is negative in the case of feedback from supervisors. These findings prompted the two investigators to conclude that 'such feedback is doing more harm than good'.

10 Despite the weak empirical support for using supervisory ratings, the courts are inclined to attach great weight to supervisory ratings as long as they are based on adequately documented classroom observations. The following sentiments expressed by one judge reflect this deference to supervisory ratings:

> Teaching is an art as well as a profession and requires a large amount of preparation in order to qualify one in that profession. The ordinary layman is not well versed in that art, neither is he in a position to measure the necessary qualifications required for the teacher of today. In our judgment this information can be imparted by one who is versed and alert in the profession and aware of the qualifications required... We think *the Principal* with the years of experience possessed by him *can be classed properly as an expert in the teaching profession, and is in a similar position as a doctor in the medical profession.* — Fowler v. Young *et al.*, Board of Education, 65 N.E. 2d 399 (1945); (my emphasis).

11 Although student ratings are seldom used to identify incompetent teachers, there are sound reasons for relying more heavily on ratings from this source. Student ratings are commonly used to evaluate the effectiveness of classroom instruction at the college level (Aleamoni, 1981). Over the past fifty years extensive research has been conducted on the reliability and validity of these ratings. This body of research provides strong empirical support for the following conclusions: (i) student ratings are highly stable (Aleamoni, 1981); (ii) they are strongly related to student achievement

(Cohen, 1981), and (iii) they are highly effective in promoting improvement within a class over the course of a semester (Cohen, 1980). This research leaves no doubt that student ratings represent a sound choice for evaluating instruction at the college level.

Research on the reliability and validity of student ratings at the elementary and secondary levels of education is much more sparse; however, the results are generally consistent with what has been found at the college level. Student ratings appear to be reliable (Bryan, 1963; Remers, 1939; Stalnecker and Remers, 1929). Similarly, student ratings are effective in fostering changes in teacher behavior and instructional improvement (Bryan, 1963; Gage and others 1960; Tuckman and Oliver, 1968). Finally, student ratings are reasonably good indicators of how much students are learning from their teachers. In the most carefully designed and comprehensive study on this issue, McCall and Krause (1959) conclude, 'The only persons in the school system who were found to be professionally competent to judge the worth (as measured by gains in achievement) of teachers were their pupils'. Two other studies (Anderson, 1954; Lins, 1946) show low, but positive correlations between student ratings of teacher effectiveness and pupil growth in achievement. On balance, the empirical case that can be made for student ratings is stronger than the one which can be made for supervisor ratings.

12 When pinpointing the reasons for a teacher's substandard performance, administrators sometimes seemed to be unaware of the importance of determining whether difficulties were due to a lack of skill or effort. The importance of this determination cannot be overstated. Difficulties attributable to lack of effort require different treatment than difficulties stemming from lack of skill (Bridges and Groves, 1990, Bridges, 1985). In determining whether the teacher's difficulties are due to a lack of effort or skill, the administrator should seek answers to the following sorts of questions: Could the teacher do what is expected if his or her life depended on it? Has the teacher ever shown in the past that (s)he is able to do what is expected? If the answers to both of these questions are yes, the teacher's difficulties probably reflect a lack of motivation or effort. If the answers are no, the difficulties in all likelihood are due to a lack of skill. The nature of the treatment should reflect the answers to these questions.

13 Kelleher (1985) reports that the incompetent teachers with whom he has worked in the state of New York often have similar troubles.

Chapter 2

Tolerance and Protection of the Poor Performer

Although this book is about incompetent teachers, it is important to recognize that poor performance is a problem facing all organizations and professions. In a study of the Fortune 500 companies, the flagships of American business and industry, 97 per cent of the responding administrators indicated that they were currently supervising an ineffective subordinate (Stoeberl and Schniederjans, 1981). This problem is felt at all levels of management — lower, middle, and upper — in these companies and is on the increase (*Ibid*). Doctors and lawyers, as well as industrial chiefs, have incompetents in their midst. Malpractice suits plague the medical profession (King, 1977), and lawyers are charged with ineffectively representing their clients (Burger, 1968; Finer, 1973). Clearly incompetence is not a problem that is limited to the teaching profession.

Moreover, the most common response to this problem in all professions, organizations, and societies is to tolerate and protect the inept (Goode, 1967). Direct confrontation of the ineffective subordinate occurs infrequently in the Fortune 500 companies; managers are far more likely to work around the problem (Stoeberl and Schneiderjans, 1981). Transfer is the dominant coping action followed by position realignment or reassignment (Stoeberl and Schneiderjans, 1981). In the medical profession when physicians are sued for malpractice, it is almost impossible to get physicians to testify against their colleagues (Vogel and Delgado, 1980). Lawyers also are loath to engage in self-regulation; when they investigate client complaints, there is a marked tendency to abandon performance standards and to search only for gross misconduct, moral guilt, or deviance (Marks and Cathcart, 1974). Only the most flagrantly inept in any organization or profession is apt to be fired or to be disciplined (Goode, 1967).

The responses of school administrators to the incompetent teacher are not much different. Many school administrators, like their counterparts in business and the more prestigious professions, are inclined to tolerate and protect the poor performer. In this chapter we will examine the factors which either reinforce or weaken these tendencies, and we will describe the various ways in which school officials tolerate, protect, and limit the destructiveness of incompetent teachers.

The Seeds of Tolerance

The inclination of administrators to tolerate and protect, rather than confront, the incompetent teacher is shaped by a combination of situational and personal factors. Two of the most important situational factors are the legal employment rights possessed by the majority of California teachers and the difficulties inherent in evaluating the competence of classroom teachers. The most important personal factor is the deeply-seated human desire to avoid the conflict and unpleasantness which often accompany criticism of others. These three factors jointly exert a potent influence on administrators to be lenient with the poor performers.

Job Security

One factor which inclines administrators to tolerate and protect the poor performer and to use the sanction of dismissal so rarely is the job security enjoyed by most classroom teachers. Nearly 80 per cent of the 180,000 teachers employed in the California public schools (California Coalition for Fair School Finance, 1984) are 'permanent' employees while the remaining teachers are either 'probationary' (approximately 13 per cent) or 'temporary' (less than 7 per cent) employees. Temporary teachers are generally hired to replace a teacher who either is on leave or has a long-term illness; they may be terminated without cause at the expiration of their contract. Probationary and permanent teachers, on the other hand, are members of a protected class and possess substantial protections against layoff or dismissal. Since the vast majority of California schoolteachers are permanent employees, let us consider the nature of the job security which this group possesses as a means of understanding why administrators are loath to dismiss incompetent teachers.

Following two years of service as a probationary employee, a teacher acquires permanent status or tenure if (s)he is employed for the third successive year in the same school district. Once teachers have attained this employment status they have the right to continued possession of their jobs. This right constitutes a property right under the Fourteenth Amendment of the United States Constitution and may be taken away only if the employer proves that there is cause for dismissal and provides the teacher with procedural due process.

There are twelve causes for dismissal specified in the California Education Code. One of these causes is incompetence; some of the other causes are immoral conduct, dishonesty, refusal to obey school laws or regulations, and alcoholic or drug abuse which makes the teacher unfit to instruct or associate with children. If incompetence is a cause for dismissal and the teacher has tenure, (s)he is presumed to be competent. The burden of proof rests on the district to prove otherwise.

In addition to dismissal for cause only, the permanent teacher is guaranteed numerous due process rights in California. For example, the teacher is entitled to the following procedural rights: (a) a written statement of the charges and the materials on which they are based; (b) access to the facts, documents, and names of witnesses to be used by the district; (c) a hearing before a three-person Commission on Professional Competence; (d) an opportunity to be represented by legal counsel; (e) an opportunity to cross-examine witnesses; and (f) an opportunity to appeal an adverse decision to the Superior Court.

These various rights create a condition of uncertainty for local school officials. There is the ever-present possibility that the Commission on Professional Competence may rule against the school district. During the three-year period 1978–80, the Commission on Professional Competence presided over ninety-one dismissal cases in California. Teachers won thirty-eight of these cases outright. The possibility of losing a case is indeed a real one for local districts.

Moreover, the tenured teacher's right to a hearing saddles the administration with heavy financial burdens. Several of the administrators whom we interviewed set aside $50,000 every time they identify a teacher who is a likely candidate for dismissal. In some cases, even this hefty amount is inadequate as the following letter from a Personnel Director indicates:

January 18 1984

Dr. William Cunningham
Assistant to the Governor for Education

Office of the Governor
State Capitol Building
Sacramento, CA 95814

Dear Dr. Cunningham:

... Over a two-year period, our costs (related to a permanent employee dismissal) have totaled $166,715. I have attached a detailed summary of the District's expenses. It is outrageous for a small school district (approximately 1100 ADA) to incur such astronomical expenses in order to remove an incompetent teacher from the classroom!

...

Sincerely,

Director of Personnel

PERMANENT CERTIFICATED DISMISSAL COSTS FOR DISTRICT

			$
1	Attorney fees		71,154.38
2	Expert witness — Curriculum		
	— Classroom observations and assistant to teacher 12/83		
	— Hearing		1,480.48
3	Expert witness — Typewriting analysis		250.00
4	Substitute teacher for dismissal teacher 1/83–1/84		15,390.00
5	Salary for dismissal teacher 1/83–1/84		26,658.23
6	Out of state witness (former Principal)		1,002.00
7	Administrative salaries (1981–82) (1982–83)		
	C__	(30% for 1 year)	9,600
	C__	(10% for 1 year)	2,700
	A__	(30% for 1/2 year)	4,995
	F__	(15% for 1/2 year)	2,175
	G__	(2% for 2 years)	1,360

S__	(3% for 2 years)	2,460	
L__	(25% for 2 years)	16,500	39,790.00*

8	Substitute for teacher panel member		
	(October 11–20 1983)	405.00	
	(December 7–10 1983)	180.00	
	Substitute for district panel member		
	(December 8 1983)	155.17	740.17*

9	Miscellaneous expense		254.69
10	Court reporter		1,975.75*
11	Exeter Memorial Bldg. (hearing location)		420.00*
12	Hearing officer (estimate)		7,600.00
			166,715.70

*Shared expenses if district wins case ($10,735.92)

If the district loses such a case (it won this one), it is also obligated to pay for the teacher's legal fees, even if the union is representing the teacher at the hearing. Dismissal of a tenured teacher for incompetence can be a costly, as well as a problematic, undertaking.

The incompetent teacher who has acquired tenure is also protected in the event of layoffs. In California, school districts possess little discretion in the reasons, timing, or manner of reducing their staffs.[1] If a district can prove that there is cause to reduce the size of its teaching force (for example, declines in enrollment or reduction of a 'particular kind of service'), seniority must be the basis for layoffs. The education code, in effect, prohibits layoffs on the basis of performance, regardless of how extreme the differences in performance may be. Seniority also dictates the order in which laid off teachers are recalled to duty. Moreover, RIF (reduction-in-force) decisions, like dismissal decisions, may be contested by teachers. In 1975, 65 per cent of the layoff decisions of local school officials were rejected in whole or in part by hearing officers (Ozsogomonyan, 1976). Clearly the need for layoffs does not provide school districts in California with an opportunity to dump the incompetents. Beyond question, poorly-performing teachers in this state are ensconced in a multi-layered legal cocoon, and this legal casing discourages administrators from confronting and dismissing these teachers.

Ambiguity in Teacher Evaluation

The ambiguity inherent in teacher evaluation and the job security of most teachers exert a powerful influence on administrators to tolerate the incompetent teacher and to avoid the use of dismissal. Although incompetence is sufficient cause for dismissing a tenured teacher, it constitutes extremely problematic grounds for challenging the tenured teacher's employment contract with the district. Incompetence is a concept with no precise meaning; moreover, there are no clear-cut standards or cut-off points which enable an administrator to say with certitude that a teacher is incompetent. This ambiguity poses a serious problem for administrators because the burden of proof falls on them to demonstrate that a teacher is incompetent. Administrators can never be confident under these conditions that a Commission on Professional Competence or a court judge will uphold their judgment.

Although the California Education Code specifies incompetence as a cause for dismissal, the term is undefined. Moreover, neither the statutes in the education code dealing with teacher evaluation, nor the case law relating to the dismissal of incompetent teachers, fully eliminates the ambiguity inherent in using incompetency as a cause for dismissal.

The California Education Code lists four criteria to be used by local school districts in evaluating teachers. These criteria are as follows:

1   Pupils' progress toward district-established standards of expected achievement at each grade level in each area of study;
2   Instructional techniques and strategies;
3   Adherence to curricular objectives; and
4   Establishment and maintenance of a suitable learning environment within the scope of the employee's responsibility.

In order to prove that a teacher fails to meet these criteria (and, therefore, presumably is incompetent), the administrator must supply numerous instances of specific acts which evince a failure to satisfy the criteria. However, it is unclear what acts will be accepted as legitimate indicators of a teacher's failure to satisfy a particular criterion. More importantly, the administrator is in the dark with respect to how many specific instances (s)he must accumulate to persuade the commission or a court judge that enough evidence exists to warrant the use of incompetence as the cause for dismissal.

Case law on the dismissal of tenured teachers for incompetence is scant in California and elsewhere (Bridges and Gumport, 1984) and does little to repair the ambiguities in the education code. According to one California court that has chosen to address the issue,

> Incompetency as a basis for dismissal does not invoke the vagueness and uncertainty of the phrases — moral turpitude, immorality, or unprofessional conduct. It is a plain word and means not competent. (*The American Heritage Dictionary of the English Language* (1981) p. 666) Competent, in turn, means properly or well qualified; capable — adequate for the purpose; suitable; sufficient (*Ibid* p. 271)... While empirical standards to measure teacher competence are not in the record before us, we have little doubt the teacher members of the Commission have the professional experience and skill meaningfully to assess teacher competence... Importantly, the concept of incompetency is not so arcane as to suggest a court is incapable of reviewing the record of administrative proceedings to determine if substantial evidence supports the agency conclusion ... incompetency supported by specific acts is a basis for dismissal.[2]

This statement on the meaning of incompetence and the manner of its determination provides virtually no clues to the administrator regarding either the operational meaning of the term or the nature and number of acts which constitute substantial evidence. Under such ambiguous conditions, one begins to understand why administrators may be reluctant to use incompetence as a cause for dismissal. The reluctance is even more understandable given the fact that one member of the three-person Commission on Professional Competence is chosen by the teacher.

Desire to Avoid Conflict and Discomfort

Individuals are predisposed to avoid unpleasantness in social encounters. They prefer to be spared the emotional ordeal entailed in criticizing and finding fault with the behavior of others. Accordingly, administrators are inclined to suffer other people's shortcomings in silence and to 'manage by guilt' (Levinson, 1964). The significant elements of management by guilt are disappointment in the employee; anger at his shortcomings; failure to confront him realistically about his job behavior; procrastination in reaching a decision about the poor performer; compliments to cover-up or ease the guilt of managerial anger; transfer to another position; and finally, discharge (Levinson, 1964). According to this view, administrators are inclined to withhold negative information from ineffective employees until the moment when termination becomes an overriding issue. As we later show, that moment rarely comes.

The organizational context in which administrators work reinforces their tendencies to suppress negative judgments. There are often contradictions between the legitimate and the expert power of the administrator; (s)he is expected to evaluate the performance of professionals whose competencies differ from his or her own (Trask, 1964). These contradictions breed self-doubt and strengthen the tendency to withhold criticism. Administrators also play multiple roles (for example, disturbance handler, 'ire' extinguisher, chaplain, resource allocator, initiator of change, ambassador, and spokesperson), and these roles limit the amount of time which administrators can spend on any one activity. Because they are unable to spend much time in a teacher's classroom, they hesitate to be critical of the teacher's performance. Moreover, criticism generates additional time demands and the need to work closely with teachers to improve their performance. Finally, lenient evaluations have functional value; they represent a potentially potent strategy for increasing the willingness of subordinates to comply with managerial initiatives (Blau, 1956). Under these conditions, the safest course of action is to follow one's instincts and avoid the conflict and discomfort that accompany confrontation.

Not surprisingly, the reluctance of administrators to confront the poor performer frequently surfaced in our interviews with school administrators. In the course of discussing how their districts deal with incompetent teachers, administrators often spoke of the principal's hesitancy in confronting the incompetent teacher. Representative comments are as follows:

> Principals gloss over problems. They only make problems for themselves by giving poor evaluations.

> About 30–45 per cent of the administrators will not confront a bad teacher and tell them that they are doing a bad job.

> Principals don't put pressure on a teacher. They would rather encourage the teacher with a good rating than make life difficult with a bad evaluation.

> Principals are reluctant to say bad things about a teacher.

The principals' reluctance to confront the weak teacher is also evident in the case histories we examined. For example,

> My predecessor was aware of the problems but never confronted the teacher.

> Her previous principals knew of the difficulties but never did anything.

> This teacher experienced difficulties for fourteen years. No one ever communicated dissatisfaction about her performance or applied pressure.

The Responses

Thus far, we have argued that the job security of teachers, the ambiguity in teacher evaluation, and the proclivities of administrators undermine their willingness to dismiss incompetent teachers and to confront them about their poor performance. In this section we will describe the ways in which administrators typically respond to the incompetent teacher. These responses reflect an inclination to tolerate and protect the inept.

Administrators manifest their tolerance and protection of the poor performer in five ways: (i) using classroom observation reports as occasions for ceremonial congratulations; (ii) using double-talk to cover their criticisms; (iii) providing inflated performance ratings; (iv) relying on escape hatches to skirt the problems; and (v) making minimal use of the sanction of dismissal. Each of these responses represents an implicit resolution to two concerns that are often in tension with one another — a concern for the welfare of the individual and a concern for the welfare of the group or the organization. The first three responses (i.e., ceremonial congratulations, double-talk, and inflated ratings) reflect an overwhelming concern for the inept employee. The fourth response, using escape hatches, continues to provide a measure of protection for the employee but minimizes, if not eliminates, the destructive consequences of the employee's ineptitude on the organization. Dismissal, the last response, reflects a dominant concern for the organization's well-being. School administrators rarely use this action to weed out the poor performers, and these individuals are usually the worst of the lot.

Using Classroom Visitations as Occasions for Ceremonial Congratulations

As a part of the teacher evaluation process, principals are required to visit classrooms and to prepare written reports of their observations. Analyses of these written accounts indicate that they are filled with glowing generalities (Guthrie and Willower, 1973). The vast majority of the statements in the observation reports are positive or laudatory in tone and contain no specific reference to what was being observed. Examples of these statements are 'I enjoyed the class', 'I was pleased with my visit', 'A good learning climate existed'. Less than 3 per cent of the statements express any criticism of the teacher and/or classroom practices. The researchers refer to these observation reports as ceremonial congratulations and maintain that such reports 'are unlikely to be a vehicle for the promotion of serious dialogue on instruction between principals and teachers' (Guthrie and Willower, 1973, p. 289).

Double-talk

Principals also manifest their tolerance for the poor performer by using double-talk to mute the criticisms in their written evaluations of teachers.[3] This tendency to deaden the sting of criticism is highlighted in the following excerpt from a training manual provided by one of the Personnel Directors whom we interviewed:

> When the famous eighteenth century French writer Voltaire said, 'Words were given to man to enable him to conceal his true feelings', he was describing a common human behavior that is far too often manifested in disciplinary documents. Instead of expressing the true facts and dealing with the problem head-on, supervisors have a tendency to pussyfoot and equivocate. This is usually rationalized as a need to be tactful and build human relations. The mollycoddling supervisor only causes a breakdown in communications... This is not to say that tact and human relations don't have a place... It is possible to be factual and direct in communicating with workers without engaging in a personal attack.

One of the ways in which principals mute their criticisms is to cast them in a positive light and to emphasize the need for continued professional growth. The 'glow and grow' approach is illustrated in the following year-end evaluation of a teacher who was under heavy fire from parents:

> Miss Jones has tried to overcome many of the complaints brought against her (actually, parents came in droves and deluged the Principal with 'I don't want my son/daughter in that classroom'). She must grow in being sensitive to the feelings of others by thinking through her statements before making them. Her attitude toward her job and her unfortunate situation has become much more positive. This attitude allows her to deal with constructive suggestions which in turn enables her to grow as a professional educator.
>
> I have enjoyed working with her and wish her success in her new position (she is being transferred). I know that a continued positive outlook and attitude toward change will only lead to her becoming a well-liked teacher. [Author's asides in parentheses.]

According to the Personnel Director, this particular teacher was

> as poor a teacher as I have ever seen. She began as a mediocre teacher and became progressively worse. The last two years were pathetic.

Another way in which principals mute their criticism is to wrap it in compliments, 'constructive' suggestions, and words of encouragement. This approach is exemplified in the following evaluation of a teacher who had been having serious discipline problems because of his unreasonable rules and harsh, military manner with students.

> Mr. Smith has continued to play an important role in volunteering to teach general science as well as his assigned math classes. He has adopted the Assertive Discipline approach in his classes. I still would like to see him relax a little more. This will take a real effort on his part because I know he cares. I believe that if he followed the Assertive Discipline approach more closely he would receive better results and be more comfortable with his students.

Inflated Ratings

In addition to using double-talk to mute their criticism, principals also show their tolerance for the poor performer by inflating the evaluations of such teachers. Inflated performance ratings are a common occurrence in the evaluations of the incompetent teachers who eventually were induced to resign their positions. Here are several examples of this practice:

> In twenty-six years he never received an unsatisfactory rating. During the past five years, he did receive a few suggestions for improvement like 'continue to be a little more low keyed' and 'if you would be a little more patient with your students you will get better results'.

> She was having problems during her probationary period and should have been terminated at that point. But, in thirteen years, she had received only one 'less than acceptable' rating — in the area 'evaluates own work'.

> Despite her shortcomings, she never received an evaluation indicating 'needs improvement' or 'unsatisfactory'. For fourteen years she was rated 'meets district's standards' in all areas.

> For fourteen years he was given a positive evaluation even though his performance was marginal.

School administrators also allude to the prevalence of inflated performance ratings when discussing the problems of dealing with incompetent teachers.

> This teacher had a history of good evaluations. This is the case 99 per cent of the time. In 99 per cent of the cases, there is no history of unsatisfactory evaluations when they come to me.

> Most often the data do not support the dismissal of an ineffective teacher because the history of evaluation is too good.

> Prior to this, no teacher in ten years had received a 'needs to improve' evaluation. Principals were extremely reluctant to give poor evaluations.

> Until a few years ago, only seven of 700 teachers received a 'needs improvement' in any area; none of the 700 was ever evaluated unsatisfactory.

This tendency towards inflated performance evaluations is not limited to California. Only 0.003 per cent of the 20,000 teachers in Baltimore, Philadelphia, and Montgomery County, Maryland, received less than a satisfactory rating in 1983 (Digilio, 1984). In

Baltimore 44.6 per cent of the teachers were rated 'outstanding' compared with 12.5 per cent of the industrial workers employed in the city (Digilio, 1984).

Escape Hatches

When an incompetent teacher begins to experience problems which can no longer be ignored, administrators may use three types of escape hatches to skirt these problems and to shield the teacher from parental criticism: (a) transfer within or between schools, (b) placement in a 'kennel', and (c) reassignment to non-teaching positions.

Transferring the teacher to another school is a favorite escape hatch[4]; nearly 70 per cent of the 141 California school districts in our statewide survey reported using this practice. The popularity of this type of transfer stems in part from the multiple purposes it serves. First and foremost, the practice takes the heat off supervisors, and spares the district from having to confront the poor performer. Second, transfer protects the district against defenses commonly used by the incompetent teacher in dismissal proceedings, namely, 'My supervisor and I had different philosophies' or 'My supervisor had it in for me'. Third, transfer is a legitimate way of ensuring that the teacher's incompetence is real and not the result of a faulty judgment by the principal. In school circles, administrators refer to this practice of transferring incompetent teachers as 'the turkey trot' or 'the dance of the lemons'. 'Frequent transfer', as one interviewee observed, 'is a strong indicator of incompetence'.

Transfer can also occur within schools as well. If the incompetent performer teaches at the junior or senior high school levels, (s)he may be switched from teaching required courses to teaching only elective courses. Although the teacher may wind up with smaller classes, the arrangement enables the school to broaden its curriculum and to provide potential complainants with a way of avoiding the weak teacher.

Placement in a 'kennel where we keep all our dogs', as one administrator termed the practice, offers a second type of escape hatch. Two such kennels are the home-teaching staff and the roving substitute pool. As a member of the home-teaching staff, the incompetent teacher works on a one-to-one basis with students in their homes. Approximately 11 per cent of the 141 districts in our statewide survey reported using this practice. As a member of the roving substitute pool, the incompetent teacher is shifted from one classroom to another on a daily basis. Nearly one-fifth of the districts in our survey reported using this practice. By using weak teachers as roving substitutes, districts solve two sets of problems at once. Since substitutes are in short supply, districts can use the rover to fill their daily needs for substitutes. Additionally, the district can avoid some of the serious problems associated with having a weak teacher in the same classroom day after day.

A third type of escape hatch entails reassignment of the incompetent teacher to a non-teaching position. In some cases, the poorly performing teacher is assigned to work in the curriculum center, the museum, the library, or the central office on a special project (for example, develop a drug abuse program, study the potential demand for driver education, and oversee the early retirement program). In other cases, the incompetent teacher is assigned the duties of a classified employee (i.e., a non-professional who is paid an hourly wage). We found instances where teachers were assigned to drive a school bus, to work in the warehouse where school supplies were stored, and to serve as a member of the building maintenance department. Administrators are not always the instigators of such assignments; sometimes the teacher who is under fire initiates the request to work as a classified employee.

Minimal Use of Dismissal

Dismissal is the harshest sanction which can be imposed on an employee and is often regarded as the corporate equivalent of the death sentence. In school districts dismissal occurs when the Board of Education acts on the recommendation of its management team to terminate the employment of a teacher and records this action in its official minutes. As a result of this action, the teacher is removed involuntarily from the district's payroll and is denied all other benefits, rights and privileges of employment. Dismissal stigmatizes the teacher and temporarily deprives him or her of the means for earning a living.

Many central office administrators expressed strong views about the use of dismissal to discipline incompetent teachers. Most administrators were extremely reluctant to issue a dismissal notice unless they were certain of winning the case if it were contested by the teacher. In the words of one Personnel Director, 'I will not carry a case to this stage (i.e., issue a notice of the intent to dismiss) unless I am confident that I can win'. A few administrators would not even consider dismissal as a possibility in dealing with the unsatisfactory teacher. One superintendent expressed his conviction this way,

> I can't imagine any circumstances where I would move to dismiss a teacher for incompetency. The law is just so difficult that it would not be worth the $100,000 plus in court fees to probably lose the case.

Other administrators objected to dismissal on humanitarian grounds; for example, a Personnel Director stated,

> We can't dismiss a teacher. We never have, and we never will. We try to encourage teachers to leave, not to kill them.

Given the expressed reluctance of administrators to discipline incompetent teachers through dismissal, it is hardly surprising to find that administrators rarely use this sanction. Over a period of nearly two years (1 September 1982 through the spring of 1984), there were 232 dismissals for incompetence in the 141 districts that participated in our statewide survey. This figure represents less than six-tenths of 1 per cent of the teachers who were employed in these districts. Although dismissal rarely occurs, its application clearly reflects the job status of teachers. Temporary teachers, as the reader may recall, can be dismissed at the expiration of their contract without cause and without benefit of due process. Even though these teachers constitute roughly 7 per cent of the California teaching force, they account for nearly 70 per cent of the total dismissals (see table 2). Conversely, tenured teachers, the ones with the greatest job security, comprise approximately 80 per cent of the work force; yet, they account for only 5.2 per cent of the total reported dismissals. The remaining dismissals (25 per cent) involve probationary teachers who possess a more limited set of protections.

The statistics in other states paint a similar picture.[5] For example, there were only eleven dismissals of tenured teachers due to incompetence that were appealed to the Pennsylvania Secretary of Education for

Table 2:   *Dismissals of Teachers by Employment Status in 141 California School Districts*

Employment Status	Percentage of Teaching Force	Number of Dismissals	Percentage of Total Dismissals
Tenured	80	12	5.2
Probationary	13	58	25.0
Temporary	7	162	69.8

adjudication between 1971 and 1976 (Finlayson, 1979). Illinois averaged ten cases annually between August 1975 and December 1979 (Thurston, 1981). Only one teacher in the state of Florida lost a teaching certificate for reason of incompetency during the 1977–78 school year (Dolgin, 1984). There is little doubt that dismissal is sparingly used with unsatisfactory teachers, particularly those with tenure, even though it is a legal cause for dismissal (Bridges and Groves, 1990).

The Factors Mitigating the Reluctance to Confront

Up to this point, we have described the various ways in which administrators respond to the incompetent teacher and discussed the situational and personal factors that incline them to tolerate and protect the ineffective teacher. There are three factors which may diminish the potentially inhibiting effects of job security, the ambiguity in teacher evaluation, and the desire of administrators to avoid conflict. These three factors are the importance attached to teacher evaluation by the district, the emergence of parental complaints, and the presence of declining enrollments. While an increased emphasis on teacher evaluation is likely to overcome the reluctance of administrators to confront the poor performers, the impact of parental complaints and declining enrollments on this tendency is conditioned by the financial health and the size of the district.

Importance Attached to Teacher Evaluation

The reluctance of administrators to confront the incompetent teacher can be overcome if a district adopts a systematic approach to teacher evaluation.[6] Unfortunately, the vast majority of school districts in California, like their counterparts elsewhere in this country, lack such an approach to teacher evaluation. In particular, they are missing three essential features of an approach that reflects a strong commitment to teacher evaluation. First, districts typically fail to provide their principals with remedial assistance that can be used in efforts to improve the performance of the unsatisfactory teacher. Even when assistance is forthcoming, it often is ineffective (Groves, 1985). Second, most districts do not provide principals with meaningful feedback, incentives, or sanctions in relation to how well they carry out their assessments of classroom teachers (*Ibid*). Third, districts rarely take steps to ensure that principals have the skills and knowledge required to evaluate teachers and to take formal action (for example, dismissal) against those who fail to improve their performance in the classroom (*Ibid*). Districts which exhibit such shortcomings in their overall approach to teacher evaluation reinforce the tolerant and protective responses of their administrators to the poor performer.

Fortunately, there are districts which have adopted policies and/or practices that are designed to heighten the administrator's concern for quality performance and to act on this concern. Some emphasize efforts to enhance the skills and motivation of principals to carry out their responsibilities for teacher evaluation. By way of illustration, one of the Personnel Directors described the efforts in his district as follows:

> Several years ago our district hired a Superintendent who was determined to get rid of poor teachers. He asked three principals to observe a master teacher in the district, and he went with them to observe this teacher. Later in a public staff meeting he asked each principal to describe what he had observed. The principals were embarrassed and started to read up on the evaluation of instruction.

> The Superintendent didn't stop there. He worked one–on–one with each principal. The two of them observed master teachers and then conferred with the teachers about their performance. At weekly management meetings we spent one hour reviewing observations. He also reviewed the written evaluations of Principals and established the norm of making fun of such statements as, 'liked by parents and faculty', 'one of my best teachers', 'great asset to my school', and 'a pleasure to have in this school'. Such statements without more are meaningless (we referred to them earlier as ceremonial congratulations). He insisted that principals should be specific and indicate why they were making these positive comments. (Author's aside in parentheses.)

With similar goals in mind, another Personnel Director tried a somewhat less threatening approach. He described it as follows:

> Nine years ago not one of our teachers was evaluated as 'unsatisfactory' in any area or category. As the new Personnel Director, I recognized that principals lacked the skills and the incentives to confront teachers. I instituted a training program

linked to the criteria we used to evaluate teachers. Principals were taught what to observe in the classroom and to prepare written reports as a follow up to the observation. During the first year principals met in groups of five to share and to criticize one another's documentation. I wasn't able to monitor these group sessions so they frequently weren't held. The following year I set aside one full day a month to deal with teacher evaluation issues, including time to consider and review documentation. Principals indicated that they didn't have time to spend working with incompetent teachers. I urged them to adopt the 'theory of one' — work closely with one teacher, assist, and document; if the teacher failed to improve, move towards dismissal. In the first year of implementation, there were twenty-eight teachers rated in 'need of improvement'. We have reached the point now where younger principals with solid training are intent on weeding out anyone who is marginal or incompetent. This presents some problems as I must set aside at least $50,000 for each teacher who may be dismissed. Very costly.

Other districts exhibit their concern for teacher quality by adopting policies and practices which discourage 'the turkey trot' or 'the dance of the lemons'. For example, in one district if a principal grants a teacher tenure and the teacher is subsequently found to be incompetent when (s)he transfers, the teacher is returned to the administrator who granted him or her tenure. In another district, the Director of Personnel monitors the annual student ratings of teachers. If a principal recommends a poorly rated teacher for transfer, the Personnel Director refuses and tells the principal to confront the problem, not to sidestep it.

Still other districts institute a comprehensive approach to teacher evaluation. The elements of one such approach are identified in the following statement by a Personnel Director whom we interviewed:

We have developed a personnel assessment manual which is used to train principals and to orient new board members. Every three to four years we conduct an inservice evaluation for our principals. Inevitably this activity boosts the number of teachers who are judged to be unsatisfactory two-fold. We have an extensive staff development program that serves the entire district and assists teachers who are in difficulty. To further overcome the reluctance of site administrators to deal with incompetent teachers, I personally meet with these teachers on the site as a show of support for the principal and as evidence of the seriousness of what's happening. I want the teacher to know that we mean business.

Twice a year we prepare a written personnel report for the board. This report lists the name of every unsatisfactory teacher, the nature of their building and teaching assignment, the nature of the teacher's difficulties, and the status of the teacher — on work plan, been issued or expect to issue a 90-day notice, or being considered for a notice of intent to dismiss. Everybody in this district knows we are serious about quality and that's the way we want it.

Districts like these pay more than lip service to teaching quality; as a consequence, their principals confront, rather than tolerate or protect, the incompetent teacher.

Complaints

The emergence of parental complaints may also stimulate the administrator to confront the poor performer. If parents choose to voice their complaints, the administrator is apt to take these complaints seriously. How seriously depends upon the manner in which they are voiced, the officials to whom the complaints are expressed, and the characteristics of the complaints and the complainants.

Assume for the moment that a child comes home and makes the following comment to her parents,

I'm not learning anything in Mr. Irish's class. He never is prepared and spends most of the period trying to get the students to pay attention. The class is a total waste of time.

Faced with this complaint from their daughter, the parents can respond in several ways. They can 'lump' it, i.e., suffer in silence and attempt to make the best of a bad situation. They can 'avoid' the source of their complaint by withdrawing their child from the school and sending her to a private school. Or, the parents can 'voice' their complaint by letting the principal know that they are dissatisfied with their daughter's teacher, Mr. Irish.

Whether these parents choose lumping, avoiding or voicing depends to some extent on their socio-economic status (SES). If they are upper-middle or middle-class and can afford a private school, they may withdraw their daughter from the public schools and enroll her in a private school. If they are middle-class parents who lack the money but care deeply about the education their daughter is receiving, they are apt to voice their complaint. If these parents belong to the lower socio-economic class, they probably will suffer in silence. Administrators are aware of these different responses by upper-middle, middle, and lower-class parents; this awareness is illustrated by these comments:

> With the lower SES group, you can get by with anything. They won't complain.

> There are no parent complaints because of the SES of our school district (low, Hispanic, transient).

> Our parents (high SES) are really savvy in educational matters and usually know what is good instruction. They won't hesitate to complain if they don't like something a teacher is doing.

If these parents choose to voice their complaint, the principal is likely to take it seriously. Parental complaints play a significant role in how principals respond to incompetent teachers. The force of these complaints in overcoming the reluctance of principals to confront the poor performers is reflected in these statements by some of the administrators whom we interviewed:

> Rarely will principals take drastic steps (initiate the dismissal process) unless they get pressure from parents.

> Parental complaints always bring the problem to a head; otherwise, principals would never do anything.

> Parent complaints are the most powerful force that we have to deal with. Without parent complaints, we leave the teacher alone. They are going to ride through.

Two of the administrators sought to explain why parental complaints can be so crucial. Their comments reveal the nature of their explanations and are reproduced below:

> Principals are apprehensive about moving against a teacher. They need a reason to act other than the teacher is incompetent because it can be very difficult to prove.

> The management of incompetence is basically a reactionary process. Supervisors have 'thousands of things to do'. With no

pressing reason to interrupt their activities, administrators simply ignore the incompetent teacher. Complaints provide the reason administrators need to go after the guy.

Even though principals are inclined to take parental complaints seriously, their effectiveness in stimulating the principal to take action depends to some extent upon their mode of expression. Voicing a complaint over the telephone appears to be the least effective. Putting the complaint in writing is more effective because written complaints reflect the intensity of the feeling about the situation. Moreover, these written complaints can be used to build a case against the teacher. These complaints typically express dissatisfaction with the teacher, offer a reason for this dissatisfaction, and request either immediate or future relief. The following examples illustrate these three features of written complaints:

Dear Principal,

This is in regards to my son, Jim Jones, going into fifth grade next year.

For his own benefit, I do not want him to have Ms. ...., Whenever I have gone to her class, it has been in a total uproar, and I feel he doesn't need to be exposed to that kind of atmosphere.

Thank you,

Mrs. Elizabeth Jones

Dear Principal,

Bob and I are very concerned about Jerry's teacher. We both do not want Jerry to continue in that class.

Mr. .... is a very nice person, but he has no class control. I have been in his class a few times, and it was a circus. We don't think Jerry is learning much in a classroom like that.

We are sure that you will take steps to see that our son is transferred. It is a difficult decision to be made, but it has to be done.

Sincerely,

Mrs. Robert Bradley

An even more effective, but seldom used, means of voicing complaints is to engage in some kind of coercive action like boycotting the teacher's classroom. Parents in one district banded together and refused to send their children to school until something was done about the incompetent teacher. This forceful action evoked an administrative response when less drastic means failed.

The effectiveness of complaints in eliciting a forthright response by the administrator also depends in part on the following factors:

1 The volume of complaints — As one administrator put it, 'An isolated complaint does not mean much as even the "best" teachers receive an occasional complaint'. On the same topic, another administrator said,

> You need a lot of external complaints to move on a teacher. The administrator is not willing to make tough decisions until he has to; that time comes when there are complaints.

2 The destination of the complaint — School districts are hierarchical organizations, and the top of the hierarchy seems to be more responsive than the bottom. In the words of a principal whom we interviewed,

> A complaint that is made in writing to the superintendent is more likely to receive attention and generate a response than a phone call to the assistant principal.

3 The originator of the complaint — If the complainant has a conduit to power (for example, is the President of the School Site Council or the friend of a Board member), the complaint is likely to be taken seriously. On the other hand, if the complainant has little or no power or is a chronic complainer, the complaint is apt to be ignored.

4 The persistence of the complainant — Staying power appears to pay dividends. In speaking to this point, one of our respondents stated,

> If a parent phones to complain about a teacher, the administrator's knee-jerk response is to say, 'Come to school where we can discuss it'. Most parents never follow through, and the matter ends there.

Successful complainants follow up and do not let the matter end so easily.

5 The nature of the complaint — Non-specific complaints are likely to be ignored. Such complaints do not contain any indication of who was involved and lack information about the time, circumstances, and nature of what happened.

6 The timing of the complaint — Administrators are inclined to discount a complaint if it is made early in the school year. 'At this time of year', one administrator noted, 'we usually tell the parent to give the teacher a chance'.

Declining Enrollments

Declines in enrollment also exert pressure on school officials to do something about incompetent teachers. If enrollments begin to decline, administrators confront the need to lay off teachers. According to the California law prevailing at the time of this study, these layoffs must be on the basis of seniority.[7] The seniority principle creates problems for administrators because incompetent teachers are much more likely to appear among the most senior segment of the teaching force than among the least senior. The likelihood of this occurrence is not due to the age or the experience of the teacher; rather, it is accounted for by the selection ratios (i.e., the proportion of applicants who were hired) in effect at the time the most experienced and least experienced teachers were employed.

Taylor and Russell's (1939) work on personnel selection clearly demonstrates that an organization's ability to screen out unsatisfactory employees at the selection stage depends in part upon the favorability of selection ratios.[8] Favorable selection ratios exist during a period of labor surplus when an organization hires only 10 to 20 per cent of the applicants. Unfavorable selection ratios occur during a period of labor shortage when an organization is forced to hire 80 to 90 per cent of the applicants. Organizations are less likely to hire individuals who later are judged unsatisfactory in a period of labor surplus than in a period of labor shortage.[9] Since the least senior teachers were hired during a period of labor surplus and the most senior teachers were hired during an era of teacher shortages — 'thirty-five applicants for thirty-four positions' as one administrator put it, the odds are that the incidence of incompetence is inversely related to seniority. The odds are further strengthened by selective attrition; there is some evidence that academically able teachers are more likely to leave teaching than the less able (Schlechty and Vance, 1981).

Therefore, decreasing staff size on the basis of seniority is likely to necessitate releasing competent teachers and retaining the incompetent teachers. If administrators choose to reduce the size of their staffs through layoffs, they may be bombarded by complaints from parents who question the wisdom of this practice. When these complaints arise, school officials may be forced to adopt a more aggressive approach to teacher evaluation. Even if parents do not mount a campaign against layoffs on the basis of seniority, administrators may anticipate that staff reductions will eventually lead to complaints from parents whose children are being taught by incompetent teachers. Wishing to avoid these complaints, administrators sometimes tighten the evaluation procedures and put pressures on these teachers to improve or to leave the district.

Although complaints and declining enrollments exert a powerful influence on school administrators, these two conditions do not inevitably result in the death of the inclination to protect the incompetent teacher. The financial health and the size of the district determine whether administrators will confront the teacher or sidestep the issue when complaints arise and/or enrollments begin to fall.

Fiscal Health[10]

If the district has adequate financial resources, administrators may evade, rather than confront, the problems created by declining enrollments and complaints. As long as money is plentiful, administrators can afford to retain all teachers and to use a variety of escape hatches to avoid parental complaints. Incompetent teachers can be assigned to elective courses with small enrollments, to tutor students in their homes, to work on special projects in the central office, and to work as a classified employee. If a district is strapped for funds, administrators lose these options and must confront the incompetent teacher.

During the 1970s many California school districts were struck by a financial squeeze and were forced to confront their incompetent teachers. Three far-reaching legal developments (Elmore and McLaughlin, 1982) altered the state's system for financing public education and contributed to this fiscal crunch. In August 1971, the California Supreme Court ruled that the system was unconstitutional because it violated the wealth-free requirement for educational spending and resulted in fiscal inequities (Serrano v. Priest). Although the court did not fashion a remedy, it held that the quality of a child's education should not depend on the fortuitous presence of valuable residential, commercial, and industrial property in the district where (s)he lives. To reduce the disparities in the state's system for financing education, the California legislature passed SB90 the following year. This bill set revenue limits on how much money districts could raise through the local property tax. It also provided for differential inflation adjustments (referred to as the squeeze factor) which slowly moved high spending and low spending districts together over time. Finally, the passage of Proposition 13 by California voters in 1978 added to the financial woes of all school districts. Proposition 13 limited taxes on residential, commercial, and business property to 1 per cent of the 1975–76 assessed market value. Moreover, it limited tax assessment increases to no more than 2 per cent a year. Strapped for funds and haunted by the spectre of skyrocketing inflation, many districts could no longer afford to hide the deadwood.

Size

The size of the district also affects how administrators respond to complaints and declining enrollments. Large districts are able to cushion the impact of declining enrollments through attrition. The teaching staff can be decreased through naturally occurring events — deaths, retirements and resignations. Large districts also are able to use between-school transfer and the roving substitute pool to avoid parental complaints. If parents complain vociferously about a particular teacher, administrators can transfer the teacher to another school site.

In trying to find a new home for the incompetent teacher, some administrators look for schools where the parents either assume that all teachers are competent professionals or simply do not care about the quality of education which their children are receiving. Schools which are perceived to fit these criteria are ones with high rates of transiency, large concentrations of low SES students, and/or substantial numbers of 'problem' students (usually found in a continuation school). If schools like these cannot be found, the district may try to effect a 'lemon exchange'. Under this arrangement, two principals, each with a poor teacher, agree to swap these teachers. The switch provides temporary relief for the principals and the teachers from the complaints. The roving substitute pool offers another avenue for avoiding parental complaints. The rover, though incompetent, is unlikely to evoke complaints because (s)he is shifted from one classroom and school to another on a daily basis. Why bother to complain about a situation that is so temporary? Besides, everyone knows that kids are inclined to fool around on days when there is a substitute. Through these various arrangements, large districts are able to sidestep the pressures engendered by declining enrollments and complaints.

Small districts are unable to escape these pressures and may be forced to confront incompetent teachers when complaints surface and enrollments start to fall. Administrators in these districts are unable to use transfer as a way of avoiding complaints. Attrition is unlikely to solve the staffing problems created by declining enrollments. Moreover, if administrators decide to lay off on the basis of seniority, their decisions are more visible and subject to challenge than the layoff decisions of administrators in larger districts. The conditions in small districts, therefore, are not conducive to tolerating and protecting the poor performer. When complaints and declining enrollments strike, administrators in these districts are more likely to communicate their dissatisfaction to incompetent teachers, attempt to help them improve their performance, and to weed them out if they fail to improve.

Summary

In this section we have discussed the inclination of various organizations and professions, including the schools, to tolerate and to protect the poor performer. This propensity manifests itself in several ways in educational institutions, namely, the use of ceremonial congratulations in classroom observation reports, the use of double-talk in written evaluations to deaden the sting of criticism, the inflation of performance ratings, the use of escape hatches, and the sparing use of dismissal. Each of these responses is reinforced by three factors that are prevalent across school districts: the job security of teachers, the ambiguity inherent in teacher evaluation, and the desire of supervisors to avoid unpleasantness in their social encounters. Three additional forces may reduce the inhibiting effects of these factors, however. These forces are the importance attached by the district to teacher evaluation, the emergence of parental complaints, and the presence of declining enrollments. While an increased emphasis on teacher evaluation is likely to overcome the tendencies of administrators to tolerate and protect the poor performer, the impact of parental complaints and declining enrollments is conditioned by the financial health and size of the district. If a district is small in size and/or is caught in a financial squeeze, administrators are likely to confront the incompetent teacher when complaints arise or enrollments fall. On the other hand, if a district is large and/or has slack financial resources, administrators may respond in a way that protects the poor performer and minimizes his/her negative impact on the organization. The major elements of this discussion are depicted in Figure 1.

Figure 1. Administrative responses to the incompetent teacher: A framework

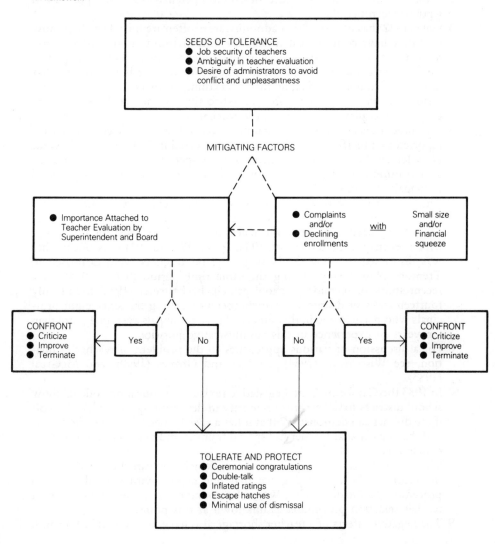

45

Edwin M. Bridges

Notes

1 Twenty states, including California, permit local school districts to lay off teachers when student enrollments decline (Zirkel and Bargerstock, 1980). Sixteen of these states regulate the order for layoffs. The vast majority of these states, including California, require districts to lay off teachers in order of inverse seniority (Zirkel and Bargerstock, 1980). In those states which do not regulate the order of teacher layoffs, local school districts still may be constrained by the collective bargaining agreement with teachers to use seniority as the basis of layoffs (Zirkel and Bargerstock, 1980).
2 Perez v. Commission on Professional Competence 149 Cal. App. 3d Cal Rptr. (December 1983).
3 Jentz (1982) has observed that administrators often are mistaken about how well they have communicated negative information to poorly performing teachers. My own experiences with students when they role play a supervisory conference with an unsatisfactory teacher is that the teacher leaves the conference feeling that everything is okay and there are no serious problems. Students are startled to receive this feedback from the persons who played the role of the teacher.
4 This practice is not new, nor is it unique to California. Fifty years ago Scott reported that inefficient teachers were transferred in Chicago and Newark, New Jersey (Scott, 1934). Transfer of incompetent teachers also appeared as a common practice in a recent study of Tennessee secondary school principals (Fournier, 1984).
5 The infrequent use of dismissal has also been documented in other states and time periods. For example, in 1927 the Chicago Superintendent of Schools reported that only ten teachers had been dismissed for any reason over a seven-year period (Scott, 1934). From 1926 to 1931 only one teacher was dismissed in Newark, New Jersey; no teachers were dismissed in Trenton, New Jersey, during the same time period (Scott, 1934). In a recent study of secondary school principals, Fournier (1984) found only fourteen cases of dismissal for incompetence among the sixty-eight principals who participated in this survey. These principals averaged more than ten years of experience in this administrative position.
6 For a discussion of various approaches to the problem of teacher evaluation, see Wise *et al.* (1984), Bridges and Groves (1990), and McGreal (1983).
7 In 1983 the California State Legislative revised the education code to allow school districts to depart from seniority in determining the order of layoff if the district can demonstrate that it has a specific need for a specific course and that a particular teacher has special training and experience to teach the course [Section 44955(d)].
8 The wider the range of applicants from which one can choose, the fewer the errors to be expected given that one begins with a valid selection procedure (Schneider, 1976). We wish to point out that the validity of most teacher selection procedures is unknown at this point.
9 The negative effects of a teacher shortage also have been noted in England.

According to Grace (1984), there was a teacher shortage in inner-city schools in the late 1960s and early 1970s. During this period, selective mechanisms appear to have weakened.

10 Between 1972 and 1982 California showed the smallest increase in total school expenditures (64.5 per cent) of any state in the union even though its enrollment declines were slightly less than the national average. During this ten-year period, per pupil expenditures also increased less in California than in any of the fifty states. Relative to other states, California ranked above the average in per pupil expenditures in 1972 and below the average ten years later.

Chapter 3

Salvage Attempts

In the previous chapter, we argued that school administrators are likely to confront the incompetent teacher if: (i) the district attaches high importance to teacher evaluation; (ii) there are parental complaints; and/or (iii) the district faces declining enrollments. Two of these conditions, parental complaints and declining enrollments, are likely to evoke a confrontational response only if the district also suffers from a financial squeeze and/or is relatively small. When administrators decide to confront the poor performer, their actions generally fall into two distinct stages: (i) how to salvage the teacher; and (ii) how to get rid of the teacher if (s)he fails to improve. The major focus of the discussion in this chapter is on stage 1, salvaging the teacher who is judged to be 'at risk' (i.e., a candidate for possible termination).

The salvage stage represents a period of unmuted criticism, defensive reaction, behavioral specification, limited assistance, restrained support, extensive documentation, and little improvement. These seven features do not constitute a set of sequential steps and may appear throughout the entire salvage stage. Moreover, these features are influenced in part by the tolerant treatment of the poor performer in the past and by the likelihood of having to terminate the teacher in the future. Let us now turn our attention to the dynamics of these salvage attempts.

Unmuted Criticism

During the salvage stage administrators abandon the practices of the earlier period. They no longer sprinkle their observation reports with glowing generalities. They no longer cloak their criticisms in the guise of constructive suggestions. They no longer inflate the evaluations of the incompetent teacher. Straight talk replaces double-talk!

Negative comments begin to creep into the observation reports prepared by supervisors. Administrators are now inclined to describe what is happening in the teacher's classroom in specific terms and to criticize the teacher's performance. By way of illustration, one principal, after making an unannounced visit, filed a written observation report containing the following comments:

Reading (9.23–10.15)

This was an unannounced visit to Ms. Kay's reading class.

The children were asked questions about 'beautifying' buildings and planting window boxes. The teacher told them that the story today was about tulips and asked them to read the story silently... After about ten minutes the children were asked to *close* their books. A few questions were asked and then they were asked to *open* their books and find the answers... This happened three times... The next activity was a short concept attainment lesson. This took about two minutes. A phonics lesson with silent 'K' in 'Kn' words was presented... At 9.50 they were asked to open their workbooks... At 10.00, the supplementary reader was passed out. The story was not completed as time ran out. Ms. Kay promised that they would complete the story another day.

Critique

... My feeling was that there was no real continuity in the lesson. Too much time was spent on opening and closing books.

There was *no* sequential discussion of the story or vocabulary drill.

The oral reading of 'Little Red Cap' was not used as an opportunity to evaluate the reading. No critiques of the reading were made. There was evidence that more oral reading experiences would be beneficial.

While this particular observation report separates the description and evaluation of what is occurring, other reports interweave these two activities but tend to emphasize the deficiencies inherent in the lesson. An example of this practice is the following supervisory report; it is based on a brief (10 minute) classroom observation:

> I observed a lesson being conducted in Mrs. Denny's classroom on Thursday 6 January from 1.20 p.m. to 1.30 p.m. The lesson was supposed to help the students learn to proofread their own work and edit their mistakes.
>
> Mrs. Denny was using the overhead projector as had been suggested to her. However, the transparency was almost illegible. We need to work with her on making readable transparencies.
>
> Mrs. Denny had not given the students any 'hands on' activity, so most of them were not paying attention. It would have been helpful if they had been given a copy of the transparency to work on at the same time.
>
> Mrs. Denny was interacting with three students who were seated nearest the board. The rest of the class was not involved.
>
> Mrs. Denny needs help in involving the students. She has a tendency to answer her own questions.

Unmuted criticism also creeps into the annual evaluations of these teachers. In fact, ratings of 'needs to improve' and 'unsatisfactory' predominate, and the most important weaknesses may even be labeled as specific incompetencies. By way of illustration, one of the teachers in our study who had been rated as outstanding, good, or satisfactory in all areas for 27 years began to receive evaluations like the following:

TEACHER EVALUATION REPORT

TEACHER'S NAME _____ DATE OBSERVED <u>18, 19 and 24 May</u> SCHOOL _____
TIME OR PERIOD OBSERVED <u>1.00–1.30–, 10.30–11.15,</u>
<u>10.40–11.10</u>

CLASS OR GRADE ___<u>5</u>___ SIZE __<u>24–26</u>__ TIME SPENT IN ROOM <u>30, 45, 30 minutes</u>

CHECK ONLY AREAS OBSERVED OR PERTINENT:

	1	2	3	4	5
CLASSROOM CONTROL					X
PLANNING AND ORGANIZATION				X	
METHODS AND TECHNIQUES				X	
KNOWLEDGE OF SUBJECT MATTER			X		
ROOM ENVIRONMENT			X		
ENTHUSIASM FOR TEACHING				X	
STUDENT RELATIONS					X
PERSONAL APPEARANCE			X		
VOICE			X		

(1 — OUTSTANDING) (2 — GOOD) (3 — SATISFACTORY) (4 — NEEDS TO IMPROVE)
(5 — UNSATISFACTORY)

1 SITUATION OBSERVED:
   15 May — Spelling lesson; also language arts
   19 May — Arithmetic lesson; also health
   24 May — Spelling lesson

2 STATEMENT OF SPECIFIC COMPETENCIES OR INCOMPETENCIES AND PERSONAL
   QUALITIES OBSERVED:
   On all three observations you did not have control of your class, in varying degrees. As many
   as six – eight students were either not paying attention, away from their desks or doing other
   work. There was too much talking going on for students to hear and concentrate. Your class
   made a slow transition from one subject to another with a resulting low level of at-task
   behavior.

3 SPECIFIC SUGGESTIONS FOR IMPROVEMENT DISCUSSED WITH THE TEACHER
   (DATE) _15 March_ (TIME) _____:
   As explained to you previously, you must have everybody's attention in order to facilitate
   learning. This may necessitate various techniques in classroom management and teaching
   which you should be able to draw from your twenty-eight years of teaching experience.

4 OTHER COMMENTS:
   Class seemed to be disorganized and displayed lack of good feeling for each other, a kind of
   low morale and poor class image which reflected itself in not paying attention to your
   instruction and disregard of your concerns for a quieter and more orderly situation.

Defensive Reactions

When confronted with criticisms of their teaching effectiveness, incompetent teachers often are defensive and antagonistic. The defensiveness and antagonism are expressed in several ways. The teachers who are under fire may deny the validity of the administrator's criticisms, may launch counter attacks, or may acknowledge their difficulties, but blame them on factors beyond their control.

For example, one teacher prepared a vigorous two-page denial of her Principal's criticisms. She challenged the accuracy of fifteen criticisms leveled by her Principal and accused him of unprofessional conduct. Excerpts from her memo are reproduced below:

To: Mr. Butterworth
From: Mrs. Little

This is to acknowledge receipt from you of the following undated documents... The information set forth ... is generally false and grossly exaggerated...

1 A There was never any problem with student/class behavioral control.

  B The quality of my student supervision has always been good and continues to be good.

  C As far as staff cooperation is concerned, I had had excellent rapport with a continually changing staff and I have not observed any problems of morale.

  D I have at all times had effective liaison with other agencies that are in contact with my class and further I have sought other agencies in order to provide a greater activity outlet for my students. All of this has been done on my initiative.

  E As to appropriate role modeling, I am unable to fathom just what, if anything, you mean by this ambiguous phrase. I do know that I set a good example of proper behavior before my students. If that is an inappropriate role model, I should like detailed enlightenment of what you mean.

  F As to student and staff safety I have no idea as to what you are talking about. I do know that no student or staff member has been injured in my class nor has there been any violence which I am sure you will acknowledge is unusual for the Blackmon site.

. . .

3 C I am an effective multi-subject teacher and I enjoy being a multi-subject teacher and I just can't understand how you could reach such an erroneous conclusion as indicated by your statement.

. . .

In any event, I had to write this letter to protect my professional reputation which you have unjustly attacked by your said notification. I like my profession and it is my career to which I am dedicated. For you to make such an unwarranted attack on me demonstrates a callous attitude not becoming a professional educator.

Another teacher responded to the unmuted criticisms of her Principal by verbally attacking him. In this particular teacher's response, she sought to portray the Principal as being unreasonable, unfair, and deceitful. The teacher also tried to discount the Principal's criticisms by raising the issue of taste and philosophical differences. Portions of this teacher's extended response are reprinted below:

> I feel Mr. Gould has been overly critical of my classroom control, teaching methods and classroom rapport... I am at a loss to explain his sudden antipathy to me. I know he himself taught in a classroom recently, and I would imagine that he would have found children's attention wandering occasionally. We all do our best to help children understand that life isn't always a TV game, and that routine lessons are like washing the dishes or cutting the lawn — something to be done carefully and as quickly as possible.

> If I were not well acquainted with Mr. Gould and know that he is of fine moral character, I might suspect that he is picking fault with insignificant little things in an effort to build a case to force my dismissal. I am putting such a thought out of my mind.

> There is one other thing that bothers me. Mr. Gould carefully told the staff at the beginning of the year that he would observe us only after having told us that he would. On none of the occasions evaluated here was I forewarned. Perhaps I could have suggested a time when something more to his liking was going on...

Even when teachers acknowledge that they are having difficulties, they may refuse to accept personal responsibility for these problems. These teachers may steadfastly maintain that 'it is the kids' fault; they aren't motivated and don't care. No one can teach under those conditions'. In some respects, the defensive responses of these poor teachers are understandable. Many of them, as we noted in the previous chapter, have been receiving satisfactory evaluations and double-talk for years. This misleading information, combined with the strong tendency of poor performers to attribute their difficulties to external causes (Mitchell, Green, and Wood, 1981), is a breeding ground for resistance and defensiveness. One interviewee summed up the problem as follows:

> It is really tough to establish a non-adversarial relationship with the incompetent teacher. As hard as we try, it is difficult, and we succeed only a small part of the time.

Behavioral Specification

Because incompetent teachers are likely to attribute their problems to external causes and to have received inaccurate information about their classroom performance prior to the salvage stage, they are apt to be unreceptive to remedial efforts. Their resistance may be further intensified by the nature of the salvage attempts. Behavioral directives constitute the core of most rescue operations and serve at least two major purposes. First, these specifications clarify where improvement is needed. Second, they ward off future contentions that the teacher never knew how his/her conduct should be improved. Unless administrators clarify how improvement will be determined, courts are likely to overturn a future dismissal decision on the grounds of insufficient notice. For example, a court that recently ruled in favor of the teacher stated:

> The warning was ... totally insufficient... The letter merely announced very tersely that improvement was needed in the areas of (1) relationship with students, (2) enthusiasm in teaching, (3) disciplinary policies, and (4) relationship with parents... Without knowledge of the specifics ..., a teacher who seeks to improve his or her teaching ability may find that such efforts result in classroom conduct that in the minds of school authorities, is even less competent, less efficient ... In short the teacher is caught in a double-bind; the teacher must improve ... or risk termination. On the other hand, there is no assurance that any particular course of action undertaken by a teacher ... will constitute sufficient improvement in the eyes of the board and school authorities. The teacher finds herself struggling blindly towards undefined and unknown standards of conduct.[1]

To assist the teacher and to avoid a reversal of a dismissal decision if one becomes necessary, school administrators spell out the tasks to be accomplished by the teacher and the classroom behaviors which should be used in achieving these goals. The behavioral specification that occurs during the salvage stage is exemplified in the following memo to one of the incompetent teachers in our sample:

Remediation Plan

1 Make a course syllabus for the entire year identifying the major topic areas to be covered (for example, chemistry,

animals, plants, etc.) and the weeks and days to be spent on each. State clearly what students are expected to learn from lessons in a way that will be clear to the student. Turn this in by 5 January. Include the number of labs, what each individual lab will be, its objectives and the due dates of the lab reports. Include on syllabus the reading assignment for each unit. Also include the dates of major quizzes and tests and the topics to be covered in each.

2   You will also need to do detailed lesson plans for each day's lesson. These should include the objectives for each day, also written out in words that can be presented to the students. The learning activities, the specific tasks that students will do to learn the material are to be listed, along with the approximate time to be spent on each. Write out the questions you will ask students. Write out how you will check to determine whether the students have in fact learned the day's lesson.

3   Participation: (a) reduce the percentage of teacher talk; (b) call on more than half of your students individually during each class period; (c) be certain that at least two-thirds to three-fourths of your students participate during each class period.

4   Target your lessons: (a) tell the students what will be covered each class period; (b) tell the students each day what they are supposed to learn (the syllabus should help); (c) tell the students what they are to have in their notes.

5   Write out your explanations and practice on a colleague.

6   Improve your question-asking skills: (a) write out your questions in advance; (b) have colleagues review them for clarity, appropriateness, and coverage; (c) show questions to the prime evaluator.

7   Diagnose and adjust: (a) you will have to develop ways to check whether the students are actually learning and when they are not, you will have to find additional ways to get them to learn; (b) give students more hand-outs, more tests

and more quizzes. There are complete unit assignment sheets which have been developed by the department. Why don't you use them?

8 Classroom control: (a) make the rules and consequences for not following them clear in advance; (b) speak to those who violate them in private first, then in public.

The behavioral specification reflected in this memo is commonplace and occurs to some extent because administrators wish to defend themselves against future charges of having been too vague about what constitutes grounds for improvement.

One of the major tools which administrators use to guide their behavioral specification is the lesson planning model of Madeline Hunter (Hunter and Russell, 1977). Since her model figures prominently in the behavioral specifications of administrators, as well as in their descriptions and evaluations of the incompetent teacher's classroom instruction, the major elements of the Hunter model are reproduced below in abbreviated form:

1 *Anticipatory Set*
An anticipatory set is an instructional activity that is designed to focus the students' attention, to provide brief practice on material which had been previously mastered, and/or to develop students' interest in the instruction which follows.

2 *The Objective and Its Purpose*
At this step of the lesson, the teacher communicates what students should be able to do when the lesson is completed and why that accomplishment is important.

3 *Instructional Input*
The instructional input phase has two components. One relates to the knowledge needed by the student to accomplish the objective while the other component relates to the means used by the teacher in presenting this information to students.

4 *Modeling*
To assist students in attaining the objective, the teacher provides examples of acceptable finished products or processes.

5 *Monitoring*
In order to determine whether students are making satisfactory progress, the teacher periodically checks for understanding. By eliciting feedback from students, teachers are able to judge whether it is necessary to modify their instruction to promote student learning.

6 *Guided Practice*

Once the teacher is reasonably sure that students possess the information and the skills needed to accomplish the objective, the teacher arranges for students to perform the complete task so that remediation can occur immediately if it is warranted. During guided practice students perform the task under the direct supervision of the teacher.

7 *Independent Practice*

As soon as students are able to perform without major errors or confusion, the teacher creates activities (usually in the form of homework assignments) for them to carry out on their own. This step is referred to as independent practice.

According to Hunter, a teacher should consider all of these steps when planning an instructional session in order to determine whether each step is necessary or appropriate for the day's lesson.

As a way of illustrating how Hunter's work colors the criticism and behavioral specification which occur during the salvage stage, we have included the following classroom observation report of a principal who has been trained to use Hunter's ideas:

Classroom Observation on 24 October 1983

This was an unannounced visit to your classroom. I arrived just as your math class was beginning.

My initial impression was that although the children knew what they were expected to do; that is, start a review paper, there was no immediate hurry on their part to do so. In fact, they chatted with their friends long after you had asked them to work quickly and quietly. The review paper was an appropriate level for review, few children had difficulty. The children that participated in the 'oral correction' of the paper gave correct and responsive answers. My only suggestion might be that the warm-up might have more of a variety of problems, or if they needed to be alike, perhaps fewer problems could give you the same information and allow for more *teaching time*. (Note: The Principal is discussing the anticipatory set and the problems that arose during this step. The behavioral specification is related to eliminating these problems.)

The 'instructional' part of the lesson was at a level far less difficult than the warm-up, and took the major part of the math period. These problems provided no challenge for your class. (Note: The Principal criticizes the teacher for selecting an inappropriate objective.)

When asking the children which operational sign they had chosen for the problem, you never asked 'why' they had chosen that sign. Particularly with subtraction children need to explain in their own words how and why they make the choice. This is a very difficult concept to master. As the teacher you need to explain 'after them' that they wanted to find the difference. This concept needs constant reinforcement. (Note: The Principal describes how the teacher handled the monitoring step and specifies the actions which the teacher should take to overcome the deficiencies he has noted.)

The homework assignment was related to what you had worked on in class, but there was really no need to give that assignment; it did not appear that anyone (except perhaps Paul Brown) needed in-depth work on that skill. I did wonder why after Paul Brown gave such a totally impossible answer to a problem, you had not checked out his mistake. (Note: The Principal criticizes the teacher for assigning inappropriate material for independent practice and for failure to perform the monitoring function effectively with one of her students.)

. . .

You are patient with your class and I do believe eager to provide them with a happy learning environment. I am concerned that your standards for behavior, content, and presentation are too low for the students that you have. I want to help you correct this. Please ask for help in anyway that would be comfortable for you. Please arrange an appointment to discuss this at your earliest convenience.

Limited Assistance

Although behavioral specification plays a dominant role in salvage attempts, it is not the only type of assistance which incompetent teachers receive during this stage. Besides a steady diet of advice, the poor performer also is offered other opportunities like observing the classrooms of outstanding teachers. When the teacher is granted these opportunities, administrators rarely take steps to facilitate the transfer of learning. Moreover, they seldom tailor the assistance to the causes of the teacher's difficulties in the classroom. The haphazard quality of these attempts to assist the teacher is due in large part to the lack of a proven technology for remediating the poor performer and to insufficient resources.

Administrators tend to rely on a common set of solutions in their efforts to improve the performance of the incompetent teacher. In addition to behavioral specification, they provide such teachers with opportunities to visit the classes of exceptional teachers, access to consultants for a short period of time, and opportunities to attend workshops, usually on assertive discipline. If the district has a staff development program, the poor performer is encouraged or required to participate in programs which are usually based on the work of Madeline Hunter. This assistance may be unaccompanied by the actions which are necessary to make it effective. For example, teachers who are encouraged to visit the classes of exceptional performers may not be prepared to take full advantage of this opportunity. Incompetent teachers require such preparation as indicated by the most thoughtful and perceptive remediator whom we interviewed:

> Marginal teachers are unable to transfer learnings from one situation to another. When you use exceptional teachers as models to demonstrate teaching techniques, you must *precede* these visits by a consideration of 'here's what to look for and to figure out why it's happening'. You must also *follow* these classroom visitations with a discussion that focuses on a particular objective. Weak teachers need several exposures to what exceptional performances might be, and these models should be with similar kinds of students at the same grade level or in the same content area.

In short, merely releasing poor teachers to visit the classrooms of strong ones is insufficient. The groundwork must be laid before and after the visitations to facilitate the transfer of learning. This seldom happens.

Administrators also may fail to tailor the remediation to the causes of the teacher's difficulties. As we indicated in the first chapter, the teacher's classroom difficulties often stem from personal disorders (for example, alcoholism, mental illness) and outside influences (for example, marital and financial difficulties), as well as skill deficiencies or lack of motivation. Yet, few districts have the capability of responding to the needs of teachers whose difficulties are attributable, at least in part, to personal disorders and outside influences. In consequence, teachers often do not receive assistance that is targeted to these problems;

instead, they receive assistance which is relevant to difficulties caused by deficiencies in skill or effort.

By way of illustration, one of the incompetent teachers in our study had been performing satisfactorily in the classroom for fifteen years. His troubles in the classroom began when his marriage fell apart. His wife divorced him to marry his 'best' friend, the person with whom he was team teaching. For several years, the teacher walked around like a 'zombie', and his health deteriorated. Discipline problems escalated, and students' performance on statewide tests dropped below school norms. During this period, the teacher was treated as though his difficulties in the classroom were due to skill deficiences. He was given advice on how to handle his classes, sent to assertive discipline workshops, encouraged to visit other classes, and provided with assistance in preparing lesson plans. Administrators apparently did not address the underlying causes of the teacher's poor performance (i.e., the trauma produced by the break-up of his marriage and the betrayal by his best friend), and he eventually was persuaded to resign.

The limited and somewhat haphazard character of efforts to remediate the poor performer is due in large part to the lack of a proven technology for diagnosing and remediating the incompetent teacher. University-based training programs have not prepared administrators to identify the causes of poor performance and to target the remediation to these causes. Moreover, educational researchers have not attempted to build the knowledge base which the administrator needs to deal effectively with the unique problems involved in remediating teachers who have been labeled unsatisfactory. As a result, administrators are placed in a position where they have to rely on trial and error methods and a limited set of solutions to salvage the poor performer.

Restrained Support

Despite the scope of their classroom difficulties, incompetent teachers are unlikely to receive much encouragement during the salvage stage. Administrators consciously withhold social support at this stage. Their response is shaped to a great extent by the possibility of future legal action against the teacher.

Teaching is an extremely complex activity, and incompetent teachers often manifest numerous shortcomings in performing this complicated task. Under such conditions, it is unrealistic to expect major changes overnight. To improve, the teacher may need to learn new sets of skills and to integrate these skills into a long-established behavior pattern. Improvement in these cases is likely to occur in small increments, rather than in giant steps. If a teacher is to attain a satisfactory level of performance, (s)he needs positive reinforcement for any behavior that moves closer and closer to the supervisor's expectations of good performance (Hersey and Blanchard, 1982). Moreover, this reinforcement should immediately follow any behavior which is in the desired direction. In other words, behavioral specification, if it is to be effective, should be accompanied by positive reinforcement of any behavior that approximates the desired performance.

Although the teacher may benefit from positive reinforcement for small amounts of progress, administrators upon advice from legal counsel are wary of providing such reinforcement during the salvage stage. If they positively reinforce the teacher for successive approximations to the desired performance, they run the risk of building a case for retention as well as for dismissal. The teacher's defense counsel can point to these praiseworthy comments as evidence of the progress which the teacher is making in becoming a satisfactory performer in the classroom. To avoid this potential trap, administrators are inclined to withhold laudatory comments regarding improvement unless it is quite pronounced. When they do use praise, it is apt to be for actions which are tangential to the teacher's deficiencies. As an additional safeguard against future legal disasters, the Personnel Director or the Attorney for the school district, may actually preview the written communications of principals to ensure that they do not contain comments which ultimately may undermine the case against the teacher.

Extensive Documentation

Perhaps the most conspicuous feature of the salvage stage is the extensive documentation which occurs during this period. This feature of salvage attempts, like unmuted criticism, behavioral specification, and restrained support, is largely influenced by the prospects of future dismissal. The more the incompetent teacher is 'at risk', the more voluminous this documentation is likely to be. In crafting this written material, administrators attempt to create a number of impressions which they deem essential to an airtight case.

To illustrate how much documentation can be accumulated during this stage, one of our informants characterized a recent salvage operation as a 'three Morgan case'. A 'Morgan' is a file box in which lawyers store their legal papers; these 'Morgans' were 15½″ long, 10½″ high, and 12¼″ wide. In this instance, each 'Morgan' was crammed full of written material about what had transpired during the remediation period.

This material included documents like the following: copies of parental complaints, reports of classroom observations, statements of deficiencies, plans of assistance (usually in the form of behavioral specification), reviews of progress, summaries of problems and actions taken, and responses (if any) of the teacher to what is occurring. Documentation like this represents a crucial component of a district's case against a teacher if the administration later decides to get rid of the incompetent teacher.

When preparing and assembling this documentation, administrators are consciously writing for two audiences. One is the incompetent teacher and the other is a future adjudicator (for example, a Commission on Professional Competence or a court judge). In the mind of the administrator, the adjudicator is often the more salient and important spectator of the two. To prepare for a possible review of their documentation by an adjudicator, administrators attempt to convey a number of impressions through their various documents. As a way of providing the reader with a concrete idea of how administrators seek to create these impressions, we have reproduced several documents relating to one of the incompetent teachers in our study. Following the presentation of these documents, we will identify what these impressions are and will show how the documentation is attempting to foster these impressions. The reader should bear in mind that the Principal who has prepared these documents possesses an exceptional level of expertise.

Report of
Classroom Observation
(December 2)

The purpose of my visit to Mr. Staley's classroom was to get an impression about his teaching on a sustained basis. I sat in the classroom from 9.00 a.m. until 12.18 p.m. I believe that in this length of time I was able to gather some information on the totality of teaching performance.

Mr. Staley's students appear to be an excellent group of pupils. They appear to be bright and eager to learn and are certainly very vociferous and rambunctious. Mr. Staley used a soft tone of voice and he was very generous with his praise to several students, reminding them of their good behavior of the day before, as well as how they should behave this particular morning.

The first thing that struck me within a few minutes in the classroom was the chaos in the classroom. As I mentioned before, the children are rambunctious and talkative. It took a long time to get them organized and going. Let me point out some areas that I think need to be seriously improved.

1   Time on Task — Throughout the time I was there one of the most serious problems I saw was the loss of instructional time. It took a very long time for Mr. Staley to get the students settled down and ready to go into the lessons. Even when the lesson was started, there was no order. Several students were still searching for materials, talking, and generally doing pretty much what they pleased. Getting ready for the reading lesson took eight minutes; getting ready for the math lesson took thirteen minutes; getting ready for the spelling lesson took several minutes, though I didn't time that particular instance.

Soon after the flag salute was done, a group got up and, after a lot of visiting along the way, left the room. (I am assuming they were going to the lab or to another reading group in another room.) It took an inordinately long time for this group to leave the room. Most of them stopped along the way to talk to their neighbors. One boy in particular had to be called back and given a lecture by the teacher in the manner in which he should leave the room. This kind of activity, again, took a long time which could well have been spent on instruction.

2   Lack of Order — If there is one thing we know about education and the teaching/learning process, it is that in order for learning to take place there has to be an orderly environment. Mr. Staley's classroom certainly is not an orderly environment where learning can be maximized. There is a lot of talking by the students, and a lot of disorganization and groping on the part of Mr. Staley. There seems to be no sense of order or purpose. During many of the lessons children continued their visitations, their

grumbling towards the teacher, their doodling, or attending to something else. Five girls emptied their desk bins of clutter and organized their desks, passing the trash can along the floor with loud popping sounds. The noise level is very high, not only with the chatter of the students, but with the banging of desk tops which appears to be very frequent and unnecessary.

3   Organization for Instruction — At the beginning of the day it appeared that there were at least two groups in reading. However, the groups were not seated in such a way as to lend to easy dialogue and interaction between the teacher and students. Groups 11 and 12 were engaged in two different types of activities, but students from both groups were intermingled so that whatever interaction took place between the teacher and the students was dispersed throughout the room creating a sense of confusion and thus the other group was unable to concentrate on the material.

By the time the students got their papers and pencils ready for the spelling lesson, about 50 per cent of the students had to go to the reading lab. The spelling was given only to about half the class that remained behind.

4   Seating Arrangement — The seating arrangement seems to me to add a great deal to the confusion. Many students' desks are joining each other, thus facilitating the visiting and chatter that characterizes the room. In addition, there are several students whose seating arrangements appear to be real serious problems. There is a student in the back, near the closet, who spent at least 90 per cent of his time writing on the wall of the closet next to his chair. He used mostly a pencil but sometimes a felt pen. At least twice during my three hours there the student got up to go to the sink, get some wet paper towels and cleaned the wall so that he could begin again on his private graffiti area next to him.

About three feet away, to this student's left, are two adjoining desks. Most of the time two girls sit at these desks and are totally oblivious to what is going on in the classroom. They were very much engrossed in each other's conversation and one of them had a pocket-type electronic game that she played with constantly, pretty much oblivious to the world around her.

There is one boy in the front who appears to be

academically ahead of the group and he pretty much worked on his own. There was some interaction between him and Mr. Staley but not of an instructional nature. The boy, more often than not, was listening to his radio with his earphones on. Between the spelling lesson and the math lesson he stapled some pictures on the bulletin board at the back of the room.

5   Control of Students — During the time I was there, Mr. Staley tried to control the students by issuing 'warnings'. Several times he would say, 'Right now, everybody is on warning'. Several times also, he made the statement, 'Everyone who is talking about now is on warning'. (This was kind of ludicrous because most of the time everybody was talking.) During the time I was there, Mr. Staley put the names of six students on the chalkboard; of the six, one had a ten after his name; one had a twenty; and one had a thirty. I am assuming that, based on our school's discipline policy, this meant that these students had detention totaling the number of minutes after their names. Since I did not stay for the end of the day, I wonder whether these students ever made up that detention or whether it was just a game. I was aware that Mr. Staley had a 3 o'clock parent conference on that day so, therefore, it would be next to impossible to have detention on that day.

6   Attention to Individual Student Performance — During the first part of the day students were supposed to have worked on their workbooks and filled in some blanks, if they had not yet done that from the previous day. Soon after this announcement was made, Mr. Staley announced that they were now going to correct the material. He asked students to read the statements with the correct answers in them. As I walked around the room to see how students were doing, there were several students who had not completed the work and who were filling in the blanks as the right answers were given. At the end of the correcting period, Mr. Staley told the students to write the number they had gotten correct at the top of the page and put a square around the number. Students who filled in the blanks as the answers were given, gave themselves full credit even though they had not done the work before the grading took place. The same was true of the grading of the spelling words after the

spelling words were given to the group that remained in the morning after several students left the room to go elsewhere. During the math lesson the students were given a long division exercise. Half of the items were single digit division problems and half the problems had double digit divisors. As I walked around the room I noticed that, by and large, the majority of the students could do the single digit division problems. However, the majority of the students had a very difficult time with the double digit divisor problems. I spot checked nine students and asked them to show me the operation of the division problems. Seven of the nine did not know how to do long division using two digits. There were several students that I also spot checked who had the correct answers but these students had calculators. When I asked these students to show me the operation without using their calculators, they were unable to do so. There was only one student who seemed to understand all the math problems. There might have been others, I did not check everyone.

As I paced through the room and stopped to observe students closely on how they were working, I got the distinct impression that they were struggling with this lesson. (This type of math appeared to me to be rather simple for sixth graders this far into the school year which concerns me.) In addition, I am not convinced that the students know their multiplication tables sufficiently well enough to do this kind of math. There was one student whom I asked to work a problem for me, 59 divided into 3200. He got the correct answer, 54 with a remainder of 14. It took him nine minutes of trial and error.

7   Insufficient Planning — After group 12 (early morning reading lesson) was finished with its lesson, Mr. Staley asked them to read, 'The Rare and Wild'. As soon as Mr. Staley turned his back to attend to other matters, the students closed their books and began visiting and doing other things. When I asked some of them why they were not reading, they claimed they had already done it and they just sat there.

After the math lesson was over those students, who had missed the spelling lesson because they went to the lab earlier in the morning, took the test but those students that had already taken the test and were finished with the math just sat and waited for that test to be completed. This created a great opportunity for talking and visiting.

As you can see from reviewing my notes, there is a lot that needs to be worked on. Where does one begin? I am recommending that attention be given to the following areas for now:

1 Establish a sense of order so that every student is attentive and attends to the task of learning.
2 Groups be separated so that more effective instruction can take place.
3 Planning be done so that activities take place within a certain time. Parameters need to be set so that students do not have to miss out on lessons when it is time for them to be at the lab or out of the room for some predetermined reason.
4 Establish a more orderly environment. Every student needs to take pride in keeping the room clean, as well as his/her own desk and area clean.

I would like to return in about three weeks (time permitting) to see if some of these suggestions have been put into effect.

Conference Summary
(January 21)

As you and I discussed at length last Wednesday 19 January there were three main concerns expressed when we met the week previous with eleven of your parents. Those concerns were as follows:

1 Lack of homework
2 Papers not corrected and/or sent home
3 Lack of discipline in the classroom.

As we discussed, you agreed to send a packet of teacher-corrected work home every Thursday beginning 20 March 1983.

We also discussed math, language and spelling as subject areas in which it would be easy to send homework. I have ordered the masters for *American Book English, Book 6*, as you requested.

Let's plan to meet again on Friday 28 January at 2.30 p.m.

Edwin M. Bridges

Summary of Problems
and Actions
(March 18)

During the past months I have observed your class informally and formally, and expressed the following concerns to you:

1 The seating arrangement in your classroom seemed to make it difficult for some students to attend to tasks;
2 The math curriculum area seemed to lack organization to ensure that each student was being challenged to their fullest; at times groups or a group of students talked and were not paying attention while a lesson was being presented; during 'work time', after lesson has been presented and work assigned, you need to circulate more to ensure students have understood the assignment and also to answer individual questions.

To date six parents and one representative of nine parents, who met in a home and discussed their concerns, have conferenced with me and stated the following concerns: lack of teacher-corrected papers returned home daily/weekly; students (second/third) expected to copy assignments into homework books and take home; work not challenging to some students — too easy math and spelling; teacher vague in parent/teacher conference about specific child; no art projects; students allowed to finish homework in class while others who had completed theirs were to read a book and wait; classroom seemed disorganized and messy; students not paying attention during teacher presentation of a lesson; no specific place to turn in homework or other assignments; students talking too much in class.

Most of the parents expressing these concerns have been in the classroom at least one time and several have assisted in class weekly or several times.

During our conferences, which have been weekly since January, we have agreed on the following solutions to these concerns:

1 The seating arrangement was to be changed so that students were not as widely dispersed with some, therefore, having to sit near the entrance of the wing.
2 Instead of using dittoes 'related' to the current math

textbook an appropriate math textbook was to be selected with the consultation of the writer. A list of each math group with the current CAT math score adjacent to each student's name was to be submitted to the writer. Specific assignments for each group will be shown to the writer weekly.

3 You will present lessons of appropriate time length and require students to pay attention.

4 In order for parents to be aware of their child's progress, you will return students work which has been corrected at least weekly.

5 Instead of having primary students copy homework assignments from the board at this time, you will hand out printed assignment sheets whenever necessary.

6 You will use the District Parent/Teacher conference form when formally conferencing with parents and will strive to be specific when discussing a student's progress or lack of progress with a parent.

7 Periodically, art projects will be planned and accomplished.

8 Students who do not complete homework or other assignments will be dealt with in a manner which is fair and just to those who completed their work.

9 A procedure for the orderly collection and return of assignments will be planned and implemented.

10 You will use the 'Assertive Discipline Procedures' with your class as agreed upon by the district staff.

In anticipation of a possible dismissal proceeding, this administrator is trying to convey a number of impressions through her extensive documentation; these impressions are as follows:

1 'I am thorough in my evaluations'. (These judgments are based on half-day observations, not 10 minute walk-throughs.)

2 'I am fair and not biased against this teacher'. (She notes the teacher's generous use of praise and presents her criticisms of the teacher in a flat, unemotional tone. She gives the teacher three weeks, maybe more, to put the suggestions into effect; in other words, she is not harassing the teacher. She is also responsive to the teacher's requests — 'I have ordered the masters for *American Book English, Book 6* as you requested'.)

3 'The teacher is incompetent'. (She identifies numerous de-

ficiencies such as 'loss of instructional time' and 'lack of order' and cites specific instances for each — for example, 'getting ready for the reading lesson took eight minutes; getting ready for the math lesson took thirteen minutes'. The Principal notes the recurring nature of these problems by referring to them again in the 21 January and 18 March memos.)

4 'The teacher's incompetence is not due to an unfavorable teaching assignment'. (The Principal refers to the students as being an 'excellent group' who 'appear to be bright and eager to learn'.)

5 'I am trying to help the teacher improve'. (She makes five recommendations in the 2 December memo, one in the 21 January memo and ten in the 18 March memo.)

6 'The solutions which I suggested are reasonable'. (She refers to agreement by the teacher with the proposed courses of action in the memos dated 21 January and 18 March.)

7 'I am not the only one who believes that the teacher is doing a poor job'. (She refers to the comments of parents who have been in the teacher's classroom; their concerns are more credible since they do not constitute hearsay evidence.)

If the teacher fails to improve during the salvage attempt and the Principal decides to move to the next stage, documentation which has been crafted to substantiate impressions like these will play a critical role in getting rid of the teacher.

Little Improvement

The final feature of salvage attempts is the limited success of these rescue efforts. There are no miracle cures for the veteran teacher who is deemed 'at risk'. The incompetent performer is not transformed into a fully satisfactory teacher. When success occurs, it is measured in inches, not yards. The distance traveled is seldom, if ever, satisfying to the supervisor or the remediator. Substantial improvement is more an illusion than a reality.

This rather dismal view of the outcomes of salvage attempts is pervasive. It is hardly surprising to hear disappointment being expressed by administrators who rely on behavioral specification and withhold support during this stage. It is also understandable to hear failure reports from administrators whose remedial efforts have been targeted solely to skill deficiencies when the teacher's difficulties stemmed in part from outside influences or personal disorders. However, it is more difficult to understand the frustration and the doubts expressed by several staff development specialists who described their approach to remediation as follows:

> When a principal refers a marginal teacher to our remediation staff, we hold a meeting with the teacher. At this first meeting we make it clear that whatever we discuss is confidential and that the staff will never provide a written or oral report of how well the teacher is doing. We then jointly set objectives in a broad area like discipline with work on related aspects such as instructional strategies.
>
> Following this planning conference, we work with the teacher a minimum of two hours, twice a week over a period of three months. We do a lot of classroom observation. All of our visits are announced in advance and last at least one hour. We immediately follow the visitation with a one hour conference.
>
> When we meet with the teacher, we give specific, non-evaluative feedback, focus on one objective, and don't over-whelm the teacher with information. During these follow-up conferences, we positively reinforce the things they are doing well. This makes it possible for the person to say, 'I'm not doing well on x, y, and z'. We raise questions about the events which we have recorded during our visit to help them see their weaknesses. We also try to stimulate them to acknowledge their weaknesses by modeling the behaviors we want to elicit. For example, we might say, 'I tried the same thing; it didn't work out for me. In fact, it was a disaster'. If we make a suggestion, we often attribute it to a source other than ourselves and encourage the teacher to judge its worth. For example, we might say, 'My aide (or another teacher) taught me this technique. It seemed like a good idea. What do you think?'
>
> Throughout this entire process, we try to be supportive and sincere. We want these teachers to know that we want them to be successful and that we will go all out to help them.

When asked to comment on their own reactions to what they were doing to help the incompetent teacher, they disclosed the following sentiments:

> It is a frustrating process for the helper. We may save the

teacher's job, but we're never sure whether it's best for kids. The teacher rarely becomes anything better than low average. The amount of time and energy to achieve this is inordinate. Observing and being supportive are really exhausting if you are making a genuine effort to salvage the teacher.

Similar sentiments were expressed by a Personnel Director who articulated his doubts this way:

Do we really want to spend a great deal of time and money on improving a teacher who will be at best just one cut above mediocre? The veteran teacher is near impossible to make a good teacher. I really question whether it's worth the grief and the aggravation.

To avoid the frustration and limited success inherent in salvage attempts, some administrators simply choose to deemphasize the remedial efforts altogether. One of the superintendents who subscribed to this point of view described remediation as follows:

Remediation burns out the staff in trying to make these people (poor teachers) better. It sets up a negative situation where the remediator becomes the guy with the black hat. We don't really emphasize remediation because we don't want marginally competent people in our district.

Summary

The salvage stage apparently produces little improvement among the veteran teachers who are identified as 'at risk'.[2] Incompetent teachers rarely, if ever, are transformed from ugly ducklings into swans. The seeds of failure are sown early in the teacher's career. Having been fed heavy doses of ceremonial congratulations and double-talk for years, the incompetent teacher becomes defensive in the face of unmuted criticism and resists the behavioral specification that accompanies this criticism. Hampered by the lack of organizational resources and an adequate technology for diagnosing and remediating the poor performer, administrators are able to provide the incompetent teacher with only limited assistance in overcoming his/her shortcomings. Moreover, the possibility of future legal action stimulates administrators to withhold the kind of support that might facilitate improvement. It also prompts them to take actions (for example, extensive documentation, criticism and behavioral specification) which are apt to intensify the teacher's anxiety and defensiveness. Even when the helping process is separated from the evaluation process, the results remain virtually the same. Success, if it occurs, seldom represents dramatic improvement.

Notes

1 Pollard v. Bd. of Educ. Reorganized School District, 533 S.W.2d 667 (1976).
2 We wish to underscore that limited improvement is a feature of salvage attempts involving veteran teachers who are deemed 'at risk' because of incompetent classroom performance. We also want to emphasize that these teachers are often the worst ones in the district. It is possible that the effectiveness of salvage attempts depends on at least three factors: (i) the severity of the incompetence; (ii) the point in the teacher's career when the incompetence is recognized and treated; and (iii) the nature of the remediation. One district which relied heavily on the training materials and ideas of Madeline Hunter to work with beginning teachers reported that this program was effective in assisting those teachers who were having difficulties in the classroom. Another district indicated that a similar program was reasonably effective (in 50 per cent of the cases) in working with unsatisfactory teachers who had less than ten years of experience. Clearly more research is needed to ascertain the effectiveness of various remediation programs in treating (a) incompetence which stems from different causes (for example, skill, effort, or outside influences); (b) incompetence which varies in severity; and (c) incompetence which is recognized and treated at different stages of a teacher's career.

Chapter 4

Induced Exits

If the incompetent teacher fails to demonstrate sufficient improvement during the salvage stage, the administrator begins to concentrate on how to get rid of the teacher. At this juncture the administrator has essentially two options: (i) attempt to dismiss the teacher; or (ii) attempt to induce the teacher to submit a resignation or to request an early retirement. The difference between these two types of terminations is by no means trivial for the incompetent teacher. Dismissal stigmatizes the teacher, while the induced resignation or early retirement offers the teacher an opportunity to record his or her termination as a voluntary exit and, thereby, avoid public humiliation and professional stigma.

Job security exerts a major influence on the nature of the termination. If the teacher can be terminated without cause and/or due process, (s)he is apt to be dismissed. As indicated earlier, temporary teachers possess virtually no job protections. Although they constitute less than 7 per cent of the teaching force in California, they account for approximately 70 per cent of the dismissals between 1 September 1982 and May 1984.[1] Contrariwise, tenured teachers are covered by a thick layer of legal protections and account for only 5 per cent of the dismissals even though they comprise 80 per cent of the work force. When tenured teachers are terminated, administrators are far more likely to rely on induced exits than on dismissal to achieve the involuntary separation. In our statewide survey of 141 school districts, respondents reported that 320 teachers had been induced to resign or to retire early due to incompetence during the two-year reporting period. We estimate that 256 of these teachers possessed tenure[2]; this figure is more than twenty times greater than the twelve formal dismissals reported during the same time period. Even so, the proportion of tenured teachers who are being weeded out of the profession on the grounds of incompetence is small — less than 1 per cent in two years.

The next chapter will center on dismissal while this chapter will focus on the dynamics of these induced exits. In an effort to illuminate this type of departure, we will consider the role of four interrelated aspects: (a) pressure, (b) negotiations, (c) unions, and (d) inducements. Although our research indicates that each of these features plays an important role in the induced exits of incompetent teachers, one particular feature appears to be of overriding significance. This feature is pressure, and it is the first one that is discussed.

Pressure

To induce exits, administrators often apply pressure on the teacher. Administrators exert this pressure by taking actions which are designed to evoke stress or feelings of discomfort and unpleasantness. This pressure may be direct or indirect. Direct pressure creates discomfort by confronting the incompetent teacher with his or her inadequacies. Indirect pressure, on the other hand, engenders stress by effecting changes in the teacher's working conditions; the administrator who exerts this type of pressure does not explicitly communicate dissatisfaction with the teacher's performance.

Indirect Pressure

Indirect pressure is not commonly used in inducing incompetent teachers to leave. However, when indirect pressure is employed, administrators are inclined to exert it by transferring teachers to undesirable teaching assignments. For example, one superintendent described this technique in the following way:

> I had been in the district one year and was in the midst of closing a school. I knew that I was going to have to lay off teachers and I didn't want those teachers to be the best ones. So I set out to try to induce some of the older teachers to retire. The first thing I did was to talk to every teacher in the district so that I could find out what they were about, including what positions they liked and didn't like. I knew that this teacher was not extremely fond of elementary school. I decided to move this

staff member (a middle school teacher) to an elementary school in an effort to get rid of him. This teacher was having problems at the beginning of the year as expected and eventually decided to ask for an early retirement. We obliged.

In another case, a principal raised the possibility of an early retirement during a casual conversation, 'John, this is a good time for you to think about early retirement. Here's an opportunity for you to leave gracefully'. (The teacher knew parents were starting to complain about him.) The teacher replied,

Early retirement doesn't make any sense at this point. I like this school and have a lot of friends on the staff. Besides, I wouldn't know what to do at home all day. Work keeps me busy.

The following year John was transferred to another site within the district and was moved from teaching at the high school level to the junior high. At that point, he chose early retirement.

Direct Pressure

Instances such as these appear to be rare; more typically, administrators use direct pressure to induce the departures of incompetent teachers. Some of the ways in which administrators exert direct pressure in ascending order of intensity are as follows:

1 Use the power of gentle persuasion

The administrator meets with the teacher, indicates that (s)he seems to be having lots of problems, and broaches the possibility of considering another line of work or an early retirement. As one of our interviewees told a poor performer, 'You seem to have lost all interest in your work and are simply going through the motions. Why don't you try another profession?'

2 Share the problem and press for action

This approach is exemplified in the following episode described by a middle school principal:

Sam, 'we' have a problem. The parents are flooding me with requests to have their children re-assigned to another teacher.

Students are complaining about your discipline and are saying that they aren't learning anything in your class. I have visited your class several times and you spend more than half of the class time on discipline and less than half of the period on instruction. This simply can't continue. What can 'we' do about it?

3 *Increase the flow of negative communications*

Administrators who use this tactic confer frequently with the incompetent teacher and bombard the poor performer with memos. Through these verbal media, the administrator communicates dissatisfaction with the teacher's performance and describes the incidents on which the criticism is based. The administrator also increases the frequency of observations and uses these as occasions for letting the teacher know where (s)he stands. Complaining parents are encouraged to put their complaints in writing and are given assistance in preparing these written complaints. These complaints are then transmitted to the teacher and placed in the teacher's personnel file.

4 *Use threat and intimidation*

The incompetent teacher who is having problems, but has never been confronted, poses special problems for administrators. In such cases the administrator may hold a conference with a teacher and state in a forceful manner,

> We are on a collision course. Up to now we have put up with your poor performance. No longer. If you don't improve, we will move towards dismissal.

5 *Give an unsatisfactory evaluation*

As mentioned earlier, inflated performance ratings are commonplace in school districts. In a climate of widespread grade inflation, an unsatisfactory evaluation is a significant event in the lives of teachers and administrators alike. The designation signals that the teacher is having serious problems in the classroom and does not meet the performance standards of the district. Such teachers may refuse to sign their Teacher Evaluation Report even when the signature merely acknowledges receipt of the document and the teacher is entitled to file a written response to the evaluation.

6 *Place the teacher on formal remediation*

Once the teacher receives an unsatisfactory evaluation, the administration is legally obligated to develop a plan of remediation and to spell out the areas of improvement. If the district has a collective bargaining agreement, it may contain provisions for a Performance Assistance Team (PAT). Since these PATs are often composed of teachers and administrators, the incompetent teacher is now publicly stigmatized. Moreover, (s)he becomes the focal point of attention and is subjected to intensive observation and assistance. The features of this remediation were discussed earlier under the salvage stage.

7 *Issue a notice of deficiency*

Before a tenured teacher can be dismissed in California, the district administration must provide the teacher with a notice of deficiency. This notice is a formal legal document which stipulates specific deficiencies in the employee's performance, allows ninety days for improvement, and indicates the administration's intention to recommend dismissal if the teacher's performance does not improve. 'Giving a 90-day notice is the hardest thing I have had to do', said one of our respondents who had issued six 90-day notices in the past four years. The impact of such notices on the teacher must be devastating. Imagine how it would feel to receive a notice like the following:

90-Day Notice

Dear Mr. Barns,

Re: Notice of Incompetency and
Unprofessional Conduct

Pursuant to Sections 44664 and 44938 of the Education Code, this letter constitutes Notice of Incompetency and Unprofessional Conduct in your performance of your duties as a certificated employee of the District. Specific instances which are the basis for this notice are set forth below.

This letter is not a dismissal notice. If you do not correct your unsatisfactory work performance, however, it will be necessary for me to recommend that you be dismissed from employment.

The documents referred to in this letter are attached in chronological order. The attached documents include your most recent Teacher Evaluation Report, dated 27 May 1982. The time period covered by this notice is limited to the 1979–80, 1980–81 and 1981–82 school years.

1   In the Teacher's Request for Assignment which you submitted in March 1980, you attributed the behavior problems that you encountered in the 1979–80 school year to the 'oppressiveness' of the DISTAR reading system. You also wrote that sixteen (approximately two-thirds) of your third-grade class needed help from the reading specialist, and you attributed this to the inefficiency of the reading program. It would appear that you have recognized serious deficiences both in the classroom behavior of your students and in the reading program in your classroom, but that you failed to accept any responsibility as the classroom teacher for these deficiencies.

2   Your Principal was informed that approximately in January 1981, you grabbed one of your girl students and shoved her against the wall when she failed to stand in the exact spot you wanted for a class photograph. (16 January 1981 Intra-District Communication from Mr. B.)

3   Your Principal was informed that approximately in January 1981, you pulled one of your girl student's hair to stop her from going into your room to get a book after school, with the result that the student went to the office crying about this incident. (16 January 1981 Intra-District Communication from Mr. B.)

4   The Assistant Superintendent was informed in March 1981 of the following concerning one of your boy students in the 1980–81 school year:

(a)   His parents had problems with you beginning in September 1980.

(b)   You would keep their son after school 45 minutes at a time without calling his mother to let her know where her son was.

(c)   The boy's mother had found it necessary on previous occasions to call the Assistant Superintendent when you had punished her son.

(d) On one occasion, you pinched the boy on his arm while the class was going to the lunchroom.

(e) On another occasion, you grabbed the boy by the mouth from behind to shut his mouth when he was trying to explain why another student was out of his seat. The parent felt that you were unable to control yourself.

(f) The boy's mother found it necessary to have a conference with you, the Principal and her son concerning an occasion on which the boy walked out of the classroom to go to the Principal's office. During the conference, you interrupted the boy and would not let him speak.

(g) You gave no homework at all.

(h) You would telephone the boy's mother repeatedly to let her know 'How bad John was for the week' until his father began answering the phone and the calls stopped. The boy's scout master and soccer coach had no behavior problems with the boy (9 March 1981, letter from Mrs. L.C.).

5 Your Principal was informed in March 1981 of the same general complaints as are set forth in paragraph 4, above (see 10 March 1981 letter from Mrs. L.C.).

6 You were notified in writing of the 9 and 10 March 1981 letters referred to in paragraphs 4 and 5 above and were further notified that you were entitled to respond in writing. You failed to submit any written response (18 March 1981 letter from A.L.).

7 Your Teacher Evaluation Report for the 1980–81 school year by M.P. indicates that your performance was 'borderline' as to items Ia (Effectiveness of Student Control), IIb (Student Relations), IIc (Parent Relations) and IIIb (Emotional Stability). The Principal wrote that you have had strained relationships with the parents of two students who questioned your teaching and handling of pupils. He wrote that your relationship with those parents and with a number of students suffered (29 April 1981, Teacher Evaluation Report by M.P.).

8 According to a 15 March 1982 classroom observation by your Principal, you were borderline satisfactory in the areas of planning and organization, methods and techniques and student relations and needed to improve in the area of

classroom control. This observation occurred during a reading assignment in your fifth-grade class. The Principal wrote that you seldom seem to capture the attention of all students; that talking and not listening were prevalent; that many students seemed unaware of how to study, organize thoughts and prepare good answers; and while students were working on their assignment, you worked on the time-line bulletin board.

The Principal further wrote that you must have the attention and quietness of the whole class or the directions, explanations and knowledge will not be understood or heard; that your students seem to need more direction and guidance from you in completing their assignment; and that, of an entire class of thirty students, only seven students had completed the assignment (15 March 1982 Teacher Observation and Documentation Worksheet by M.P.).

9   Your Principal was informed that on or about 20 April 1982 you slapped one of your boy students across the face. In a conference with your Principal, you confirmed that you had done so. Your Principal reminded you in writing that no type of corporal punishment, or physical handling of students is allowed except where student safety is concerned (21 April 1982 Intra-District Communication from M.P.).

10 The Director of Personnel was informed of the following by the parents of a boy student in your fifth grade class in the 1980–81 school year:

> That you had called the boy 'stupid' at the beginning
> of the school year; that there was a lack of discipline
> in the classroom; that there was a lack of meaningful
> work assignments; and that the fifth grade school
> year for their son was 'very unproductive' (16 May
> 1982 letter from Mr. and Mrs. M.A.C.).

11 Your Principal observed your classroom on 18 May, 19 May and 24 May 1982. This is a fifth grade class with a class size ranging between twenty-four and twenty-six. On those occasions, he spent 30, 45 and 30 minutes respectively in your classroom.

On 18 May he observed spelling and language art lessons; on 19 May he observed arithmetic and health lessons; and on 24 May he observed a spelling lesson. He has reported as follows:

On all three observations, you did not have control of your class. As many as six — eight students were not paying attention or were away from their desks, or were doing other work. There was too much talking going on for students to hear and concentrate. Your class makes a slow transition from one subject to another with a resulting low level of at-task behavior.

The Principal also observed that the class seemed to be disorganized, and that the students displayed a lack of good feeling for each other, a low morale and a poor class image which reflected itself in the students not paying attention to your instructions and disregarding your concerns for a quieter and more orderly classroom.

12   As of the date of this notice, your Principal has received letters from eleven parents who request that their children not be placed in your class next year. These letters, copies of which are attached, are from the following persons:

(a)   L.D.
(b)   J.J.
(c)   J.K.
(d)   L.L.
(e)   O.J.
(f)   S.B.
(g)   Mr. and Mrs. G.R.
(h)   J.R.
(i)   K.B.
(j)   N.P.
(k)   M.A.P.

The reasons for these requests as set forth in the above letters include, but are not limited to the following:

That there is a lack of strict discipline and firm control in your classroom (L.D.); that you do not provide adequate guidance and discipline (J.K.); that students in your class learn very little (L.L.); that you have no class control and that your classroom is a 'circus' (O.J.); that your classroom is always in turmoil; that your classroom is not a good learning atmosphere; and that you have mishandled children (K.B.).

13   In your Teacher Evaluation Report for the 1981–82 school

year, your Principal evaluated you as needing to improve in each of the following areas: Ib (Planning and Organization); Ic (Methods and Techniques); If (Student Progress); and IIc (Parent Relations).

He evaluated you as unsatisfactory in each of the following areas: Ia (Effectiveness of Student Control); and IIb (Student Relations).

In his evaluation, the Principal wrote that your ability to control the students has actually steadily declined; that you refer more students to the office for disciplinary reasons than any other teachers, or combination of teachers on the faculty; that you have been counseled to refrain from placing your hands on children but continue to violate district policy in this respect; that you need to improve your relationships with both students and parents and that, as of the date of the evaluation, six parents had requested that their children not be assigned to your classroom for 1982–83 (27 May 1982 Teacher Evaluation Report by M.P.).

The matters set forth above demonstrate incompetency in your performance of your duties as a teacher in this district. The matters relating to grabbing students, shoving a student, pulling a student's hair, keeping a student late without notifying his parents, and slapping a student, also constitute unprofessional conduct.

A copy of this notice and the attached documents will be filed in your personnel file. You are entitled to review and comment upon this notice and to have your own written comments attached. Any such written comments should be submitted to me on or before 2 July 1982.

Very truly yours,
Superintendent

ABC:sr
Encls.

8   Issue a notice of intent to dismiss

The most intense form of pressure is the issuance of a legal document from the Board of Education indicating its intention to dismiss the teacher. This document must be preceded by a 90-day notice of deficiency. It contains a statement of specific charges and the reasons for dismissal and notifies the teacher of his or her right to request a hearing and to be represented by counsel in this proceeding. In some cases, the administration will indicate that a notice has been authorized by the Board of Education and will be issued in the near future unless the teacher can think of other ways (s)he wants the situation handled (preferably a resignation or an early retirement).

The Need for Intense Pressure

The induced exit does not afford an easy avenue for getting rid of incompetent teachers; intense pressure is usually required. The power of gentle persuasion, i.e., suggesting a resignation or early retirement, does not seem to work unless it is accompanied by indirect pressure or a form of direct pressure that is of higher intensity. Although early retirements apparently are obtained with less pressure than resignations, early retirements rarely occur unless the administrator exerts pressure on the teacher to improve a performance that is explicitly labeled as deficient in one or more respects. If the teacher has not reached early retirement age, the administrator generally must issue a notice of deficiency before the teacher will submit a resignation. In a few cases, the poor performer will not agree to leave until the district prepares and issues a notice of its intent to dismiss. The road to induced exits is paved with emotional and procedural cobblestones and produces a bumpy, taxing ride for administrators and teachers alike.

Negotiations

Induced exits typically involve negotiations as well as pressure. All but six of the thirty induced exits were preceded by negotiations. The purpose of these negotiations was to exchange ideas about the terms of the separation and to reach a settlement. In the majority of these cases, administrators initiated these negotiations, and the character of these sessions was defined largely by the role adopted by the administrator: rescuer, counselor, parent, or intimidator. When teachers initiated the negotiations, they generally were accompanied by an explicit set of demands. The 'reasonableness' of these demands determined how administrators responded to them.

Administrator Initiated Negotiations

Administrators occasionally play the role of rescuer when negotiating induced exits. The rescuer presents her/himself as a Good Samaritan who will provide the embattled teacher with a way out of a potentially disastrous situation. In actuality, the administrator feigns assistance and uses a bluff to secure the teacher's resignation. By way of illustration, one Personnel Director described the following incident:

> For years we had been trying to get rid of this teacher. One evening my phone rang. It was an irate father who claimed that he had found the teacher in bed with his teenage daughter. I asked him if he intended to press charges, and he said, 'No, I don't want the publicity'. I then asked him if he would be willing to let me tell the teacher that he (the father) was going to press charges but that I might be able to get him (the teacher) off the hook if he would agree to resign. The father went along with the idea. I met with the teacher and got his resignation in 24 hours.

When negotiating an induced exit, an administrator may also seek to minimize, if not eliminate, the adversarial nature of most negotiations by acting as a counselor. The administrator as counselor is sympathetic to the plight of the teacher and attempts to discover and meet his or her needs. One of the ways in which administrators play the role of counselor is as follows:

> If the teacher is at or near retirement, I ask my staff to prepare a ballpark retirement figure based on the State Teachers' Retirement System. I then go over the teacher's retirement package with him and try to find out how much money he needs over the short-run (three-five years) and the long-run (six years and beyond). I know how much this teacher costs in wages, benefits, and absenteeism so I can compare these costs against the costs of a replacement. These replacement costs vary because we don't always replace a veteran with a beginner. The difference between the two types of costs (current and replacement) dictates the leeway I have to fashion a settlement. This amount and the teacher's needs determine what the teacher receives.

Although the teacher may be under pressure to improve his or her performance, the counselor is not the source of the pressure. Moreover, the counselor is making a genuine attempt to discover and fulfill some of the incompetent teacher's needs.

If the administrator chooses to conduct the negotiations in the role of parent, (s)he lays the cards on the table, advises the teacher to take a particular course of action, and offers assistance. In effect, the administrator says, 'I know what is best for you and for the organization. Do what I tell you and I'll help. If you don't, be prepared to suffer the consequences'. The parental approach is reflected in this administrator's description of how he negotiated a resignation of an incompetent teacher on his staff:

> Five days before the expiration of the 90-day notice, I met one-on-one with this teacher and had a heart-to-heart talk. I told him that he hadn't improved and he should pursue another line of work. I encouraged him to think about it and talk with the Teacher Rep. If he decided to resign, we would provide him with time off at full pay to look for another job and the assistance of an outplacement counselor. On the other hand, if he didn't resign, we meant business and were prepared to move toward dismissal.

The parent prides himself or herself on being fair, ethical, and compassionate (i.e., willing to pull back if the teacher is suicidal and cannot face what is happening).

The administrator as intimidator negotiates from a position of strength but is willing to strike a bargain. The intimidator reveals his intentions, buttresses his threats with factual information, and invites the teacher to suggest other alternatives. The forcefulness of the intimidator is exemplified in the words of this superintendent:

> If a teacher does not improve after a 90-day notice, I meet with the attorney and ask him what our chances of winning are. If it's less than 30 per cent, I may delay and obtain more documentation. If the chances are more favorable, I meet with the Board and ask the members if they want to issue a dismissal notice. To be sure they are behind me, I request a formal vote. After the dismissal notice is prepared, I phone the teacher and arrange a meeting two weeks hence. I indicate the topic of discussion and let the teacher sweat it out. At the meeting, I review the contents of the dismissal notice, spell out what I intend to do, and invite the teacher to suggest alternatives by asking, 'What do you want us to do?' If the teacher makes a reasonable

suggestion, I indicate that something can probably be worked out. I also advise her not to rush into it because I want to avoid accusations that I pressured her to resign. At that point, the Teacher Rep and the teacher usually request a recess. When the Teacher Rep returns, she indicates that the teacher is willing to resign if we do (a) (b) and (c). I agree if the request is reasonable and again urge the teacher to take all the time she needs and to be sure that's what she wants. When the letter of resignation is submitted, the Board rescinds its action.

The role which is actually adopted by the administrator during these negotiations depends in part on two factors: (i) the administrator's values and beliefs; and (ii) the strength of the district's case against the teacher. Some administrators express beliefs and values which incline them toward the counselor or parent roles in negotiations. For example, one superintendent expressed her philosophy as follows, 'It is most important to know what the employee's needs are and what the district can do to meet these needs'. In a similar vein, a principal commented,

> You need to find out what the teacher's goals are and balance these against the district's goals. Options must be explored in a non-adversarial situation. You should not rob the person of face and human dignity.

Other administrators seemed to be hard-liners; one of them described what it takes to deal with incompetent teachers in the following terms,

> You need a strong ego and the conviction you are on the right track. Expect to be called inhuman, a maniac, and not to be trusted. Expect teachers to view 'you' as the problem, not the teacher under fire. It comes with the territory.

Administrators with expectations and beliefs like these either adopted the role of intimidator or refused to negotiate.

The strength of the district's case against the incompetent teacher may override the administrator's beliefs and values, however. If the case is weak, i.e., there is little documentation[3], and the district wants a resignation, the administrator is likely to adopt a counselor role. On the other hand, if the case is strong, the administrator is more likely to adopt the parent or intimidator role.

Teacher-Initiated Negotiations

Teachers, as well as administrators, initiate negotiations although with somewhat less frequency. When the teacher initiates the negotiations, (s)he is usually under intense pressure, having received either a 90-day notice (notice of deficiency or incompetency) or a notice of intent to dismiss. The teacher often commences the negotiations by indicating a willingness to resign or to retire early if the district will meet certain demands. If the administration considers the demands to be reasonable, it accepts the offer as presented. On the other hand, if the administration judges any or all of the demands to be unreasonable, it will generally make a counter offer. The tests of reasonableness against which a teacher's demands are compared appear to be as follows:

1 Does the demand represent a need or a want, an apparent necessity or a frivolous desire?
2 Does the district have the funds to meet the teacher's demand?
3 Does the demand represent a legitimate claim (i.e., is it legal for the district to do what the teacher is demanding)?
4 Does the action violate the administrator's personal sense of right and wrong?

To illustrate how the answers to these questions are reflected in an administrator's response to a teacher who has initiated negotiations leading to an early retirement, let us examine the case of one of the teachers who was experiencing serious problems in her classroom.

In late March Ms. Jones submits a letter indicating a willingness to retire early if the district will do the following: (a) retain her as a consultant for the next five years (teacher will work twenty-five days per year at a rate of $5000 annually); (b) relieve her of all duties, immediately, including the need to grade the papers now in her possession; (c) place her on Industrial Accident and Illness leave for the next sixty days at full pay; (d) release her at full pay for the three remaining days of the school year; (e) pay her Blue Cross health plan until age 70 (now 59); (f) pay her dental plan until age 65; (g) remove all evaluations from her personnel file; (h) supply a strong recommendation to future employers; (i) provide retraining at district expense for her to learn word processing and computers; and (j) pay for a two-week stay at a health resort and spa in Ojai, California (second choices were Baja and St. Helena).

The Personnel Director made a counter offer to this proposal and agreed to grant the following concessions: (a) provide paid leave — either Industrial Accident or sick leave — for the balance of the semester (a legitimate need because the teacher had been injured by an unruly student in her class while school was in session); (b) pay for Blue Cross coverage until age 65 unless the teacher accepts full-time employment and is covered by a new employer (teacher does have the need for health care which district should meet if teacher remains unemployed); (c) drop the current personnel evaluation as it has not been completed (illegal to remove previous evaluations); and (d) supply letters of recommendation for business, not teaching, positions that praise her loyalty, conscientiousness, and cooperative attitude (all accurate representations). Needless to say, Ms. Jones did not receive her two-week paid vacation nor any of the other demands which the Personnel Director judged to be frivolous desires rather than genuine needs.

Unions

All of the teachers in our study who were induced to resign or to retire early worked in unionized school districts. The vast majority of these teachers belonged to the union; however, they were rank-and-file members, not union officials. Since unions are often criticized for protecting the deadwood, the role played by unions in the induced exits of incompetent teachers is of special interest. Are unions staunch defenders of the inept? Are they passive bystanders? Or are unions silent allies of the administration as it attempts to get rid of incompetent teachers via induced resignations or early retirements?

The Union's Dilemma

In responding to the poor performers in the profession, teacher unions are impaled on the horns of a dilemma. On the one hand, unions are conscious of their public image and do not want to be viewed as protectors of incompetent teachers. Furthermore, many members of the union are troubled by the presence of such teachers and believe that they should not be tolerated (Johnson, 1984). Finally, the unions have limited treasuries which can quickly be depleted by such costly actions as filing grievances, taking them to binding arbitration, and defending the deadwood against charges of incompetence.

On the other hand, teacher unions, like administrators, operate in a legal environment that has implications for how they too can respond to the shortcomings of teachers. According to several rulings of the United States Supreme Court[4], unions *owe* their members the duty of fair representation. Moreover, any member of the bargaining unit, whether (s)he belongs to the union or not, has the right to sue and recover punitive damages if the union fails to fulfill its duty of fair representation.

The standards for judging whether a union has fulfilled this duty are ambiguous and incomplete, however (Summers, 1977); and this ambiguity may deter unions from cleansing their ranks. On the subject of fair representation the Court has simply stated that a union is obligated to 'serve the interests of all members without hostility or discrimination toward any, to exercise its discretion with complete faith and honesty, and to avoid arbitrary conduct'.[5] This ruling does not obligate unions to carry every grievance to arbitration; they can 'sift out grievances that are trivial or lacking in merit' (*Ibid*). Nonetheless, unions serving blue-collar workers seem reluctant to screen out such grievances and are taking these cases to arbitration more frequently (Rabin, 1977). Leaders of teacher unions similarly recognize their vulnerability to suits for failing to represent the members of their bargaining units fairly (Johnson, 1984). These officials may be loath to cooperate with administrators in getting rid of incompetent teachers.

The Union's Role

Several administrators spoke of the protective posture of teacher unions and the problems which they pose in dealing with poor teachers. One administrator complained about the restrictions on teacher evaluation which had been negotiated by the union in his district,

> Our union contract makes it difficult to get rid of teachers. The evaluator must announce every visit in advance; only those visits may be used in the evaluation. The union will file grievances if the district tries to fire a teacher.

Another administrator, cognizant of the union's plight, characterized the union's role in these terms, 'The CTA has to defend the union member to the hilt because they can be sued for not faithfully representing their membership'. Speaking on the same issue, a third administrator stated bitterly,

> In evaluation grievances, the union may support us when the door is closed, but they always take the case to the third level (binding arbitration) whether it is warranted or not. They do this even if they know the teacher is terrible. They are not obligated to take the side of every member in every case.

Such views were in the minority, however. Most administrators spoke about the constructive role of unions in inducing incompetent teachers to resign. Some of these administrators referred to the union's assistance when discussing the process by which incompetent teachers were induced to resign. One of these administrators described the union's role in this process as follows:

> The union's role is critical in counseling a teacher out. Of the 5 per cent that get counseled out, 75 per cent are with the help of the union.

In the same vein, another administrator declared,

> I have a good relationship with the district rep, and he helps me work out programs of resignation for the poor teachers in this district. Without him, my job would be far more difficult.

Still yet another administrator described the cooperative role of the union as follows:

> CTA has been very helpful in this district at getting a teacher to resign. They provide constructive assistance to help him improve and tell him, 'You are going to have to make some adjustments in your teaching, or quit. The district will follow through (move towards dismissal) if you don't.'

Most administrators, however, revealed the union's supportive role when describing how a particular teacher was induced to resign. They often referred to the union's role as advising or persuading the teacher to quit. Only two administrators specified how the unions carried out this role. One administrator indicated that 'the teacher rep showed the teacher the figures and explained how it was in her best interests to retire' while the other administrator said that the union 'advised him (the teacher) to resign because the district had too strong a case against him'. In the bulk of the cases, the union's approach was not specified.

Since administrators are conscious of the assistance that may be provided by the teachers' union in inducing an incompetent teacher to leave the district, they solicit this cooperation in a variety of ways. A personnel director made the point forcefully: 'One of my main duties is to convince the teacher rep that this teacher does not belong in the classroom and that I have the evidence to prove it'. He and others like him use documentation of the teacher's classroom deficiences to secure the union's assistance. Other administrators seem to concentrate on cultivating a cooperative relationship with the union rep by involving him or her early in the process. A personnel director who uses this approach described it as follows:

> Whenever a teacher starts to have problems, I notify the CTA Rep and let him know that I'm not sure at this point how it will work out. I invite the Rep to check periodically with me about how the situation is progressing and to consider how and if he'd like to be of assistance.

Administrators also invite union officials to visit the classrooms of incompetent teachers. A personnel administrator who acknowledged sparing use of this practice described the following episode:

> I talked with the AFT President and told him that Miss 'X' was having serious problems. I asked him to observe her. The President went for two visits and each time left after twenty minutes because he couldn't endure what was happening. He agreed to assist in securing the resignation.

The union's role in inducing teachers to resign is not totally reactive and limited to assisting administrators. One personnel director described the quiet, unheralded efforts of a union official in her district to get rid of the deadwood as follows:

> The local teacher organization has a retirement counselor who identifies marginal teachers at or near early retirement age. He invites these teachers to meet with him to review their status in relation to retirement. He raises the possibility of early retirement and pursuing other lines of work. He also provides assistance.

We do not know whether this practice is an isolated instance; nor do we know if teacher unions are using other 'invisible' practices to police their profession.

Inducements

The vast majority of the incompetent teachers (75 per cent) in our study who resigned or retired early received inducements in exchange for their 'voluntary' separations. The inducements which a teacher actually received depended in large part upon three factors: (i) the presence of negotiations; (ii) the characteristics of the teacher (age, health, and effort); and (iii) the financial status of the district. Although administrators apparently attempted to meet some of the separated teachers' needs through various types of inducements, few teachers received settlements that matched the savings realized by districts when the teachers were terminated.

Types of Inducements

Districts offer a wide array of inducements to poor performers for their resignations and early retirements. These inducements may come in the form of administrative actions, fringe benefits, cash settlements, future employment, and outplacement counseling. Examples of each of these five different types of inducements appear in table 3.

Districts do not offer these inducements with equal frequency, however (see table 4). According to the statewide survey, the most prevalent inducement is medical coverage. Nearly one-half of the school districts offer this coverage in exchange for a resignation or an early retirement. Our interview study suggests that the coverage expires at age 65; in only one instance did the teacher receive life-time coverage. The second most common inducement is employment as a non-teaching consultant (36.9 per cent); teachers typically receive $5000 per year in this capacity and work for 25 days.[6] These consultancies never last for more than five years. Cash settlements are in third place (27 per cent). The settlements range between $5000 and $15,000. Although these cash settlements generally come without restrictions, one teacher received $7500 that could be used only to pay for the psychiatric treatment which he had been receiving. Districts rarely provide inducements to teachers in the form of assistance to pursue other careers. Less than 5 per cent of the districts furnish outplacement counseling and an even smaller proportion (less than 1 per cent) pay for training.

Table 3:   District inducements to incompetent teachers

Administrative actions
  Remove negative information from the personnel file
  Provide favorable recommendations for non-teaching positions
  Support disability claim.
  Terminate evaluation process
  Drop charges
  Drop 90-day notice
  Drop most recent formal evaluation
  Extend early retirement deadline
  Announce resignation after school year

Fringe benefits
  Medical coverage
  Paid leave for part of school year
  Supplement to state pension
  Life insurance
  Additional years of service credit toward retirement

Cash settlement
  Lump sum payment without restrictions
  Lump sum payment with restrictions

Future employment with district
  Consultant
  Substitute teacher
  Classified employee
  Half-time employment as a teacher

Outplacement counseling
  Professional assistance in preparing resumés, creating job search plans, and/or preparing for
  job interviews

Table 4:   Prevalence of inducements across California school districts (n = 141)

Inducement	Percentage of districts reporting use
Medical coverage	46.0
Employment as consultant	36.9
Cash settlement	27.0
Employment as substitute teacher	21.3
Paid leave for part of school-year	19.9
Removal of negative information from personnel file	12.8
Favorable recommendations for non-teaching positions	10.6
Supplement to the state pension	7.8
Outplacement counseling	4.3
Life insurance with a cash reserve	2.8
Employment as a 'classified' employee	2.1
Training to pursue another career	0.7

The Inducements and their Determinants

Whether a teacher receives anything in exchange for a resignation or an
early retirement depends upon the existence of negotiations. In six of

the thirty induced exits, no negotiations preceded the separation. None of these six teachers received any type of inducement other than the opportunity to have their departures recorded as resignations or early retirements. On the other hand, twenty-three of the twenty-four teachers who left following a period of negotiations received one or more of the inducements which were cited in table 3.

If the teacher receives inducements as the result of negotiations, his or her health status affects the nature of the inducements which (s)he obtains. 'Troubles with the boss' represent a stressful life event and lead to disease and illness (Holmes and Masuda, 1974). Not surprisingly, half of the teachers who were under pressure to improve their performance suffered from physical and/or mental problems. All of these teachers reached separation agreements that reflected their health difficulties. Typically the inducement was in the form of medical coverage. Occasionally, the settlement provided for cash to cover medical expenses, paid sick leave for the balance of the school year, or support of the teacher's disability claim.

The teacher's age also affects what the teacher receives in return for his or her departure; age operates primarily in relation to induced early retirements. To understand how age figures in early retirements, one needs a brief overview of the California teacher retirement system. A teacher with five years of credited service in the State Teachers' Retirement System (STRS) may retire with full benefits at age 60. Eligibility for early retirement occurs at age 55; however, the retiree's retirement allowance is reduced at the rate of 0.5 per cent for each month the early retiree is under the age of 60. For example, a teacher who retires on his fifty-ninth birthday (twelve months early) receives 94 per cent of the normal retirement allowance while a teacher who retires on his or her fifty-fifth birthday (sixty months early) receives 70 per cent. School districts are empowered to retain early retirees under a consulting contract; teachers generally receive around $5000 per year while employed in this capacity.

School districts offer three kinds of inducements to incompetent teachers to cushion the impact of early retirement. The most common practice is to employ the teacher as a paid consultant; the duration of the employment is primarily dictated by the age of the teacher in relation to normal retirement age (60). For every year under age 60, the teacher ordinarily receives a one-year consultancy at the rate of $5000 per year. A second way districts soften the financial impact of early retirement is to purchase additional years of service credit for the early retiree to enable the teacher to receive the retirement allowance of a person at age

60. The third way districts cut the costs of early retirement is through life insurance plans which enable married teachers to avoid taking a reduced pension in order to provide income for a surviving spouse.

Administrators generally view these inducements as a win–win situation. The district benefits by getting rid of the incompetent teacher, by saving money in salaries and legal fees, and by avoiding the unpleasantness and uncertainties of a hearing. The teacher wins by retaining much of what (s)he would have received if (s)he would have retired at age 60 and by escaping the humiliation of an incompetency hearing. Despite the fairly widespread use of such inducements in connection with the early retirements of incompetent teachers, the practice is not without its detractors. As one personnel director put it,

> I'm reluctant to use early retirement with incompetent teachers because it adversely affects really good teachers. It stigmatizes them and robs them of their dignity. If an incompetent teacher requests early retirement, I tell him, 'No, you haven't done a good job, and we're not going to reward you by permitting you to participate in our early retirement program'.

This administrator's point of view is rare.

In addition to health status and age, the effort of the incompetent teacher appears to influence the inducements offered in connection with a resignation or an early retirement. If the teacher is perceived to have a good attitude and to be making an all-out effort, (s)he is likely to receive a larger settlement than a teacher who has a bad attitude and is not really trying. In the handful of cases where teachers are unable to handle a classroom effectively but are perceived to be highly motivated, they seem to obtain relatively favorable settlements.[7] The extent of these settlements depends in part on the economic circumstances of the district. A district that is not being squeezed financially is more likely to offer expensive inducements than one that is financially strapped.

Although these various factors (negotiations, district wealth, and the teacher's age, health status, and effort) often account for the inducements received by incompetent teachers, these factors are not the only ones. To some extent, each induced exit has a character of its own and reflects a creative response to the personal and situational circumstances operating at the time. The following case exemplifies the tailoring that occurs in the process of inducing incompetent teachers to leave the classroom:

> Mr. Blum, age 52, teaches high school math and industrial arts in a small, relatively well-off, upper-middle class suburban

community. He is the only teacher in the math department who did not major in math at college. The performance of his students on math tests is the lowest in the department. Mr. Blum is a hard worker but is unable to maintain discipline. He sets unreasonable rules and spends an excessive amount of class time on trying to enforce these rules.

Parents are inundating the Principal with requests to have their children transferred. The Principal confronts Mr. Blum about the parental requests. His first reaction is defensiveness. Later he acknowledges that he may be burned out and expresses a willingness to consider other alternatives. Over a period of several weeks, he explores these possibilities with the Superintendent. Mr. Blum eventually agrees to enter the early retirement program three years hence. In the interim period, he agrees to serve as a classified employee. He will be employed in the building and grounds department as a craft maintenance worker. His salary and benefits will be identical to what he would have received as a classroom teacher, including any wage increases granted to teachers during this period. However, he will work twelve months rather than nine months a year.

In this example, there are a number of factors which affect the terms of the settlement. First, the teacher is age 52; as a consequence, he is not eligible for early retirement until three years hence. Second, he has a good attitude and is a conscientious employee. Third, his training in industrial arts equips him with skills which can be used in the building and grounds department. Fourth, he is willing to accept this assignment and views it as an opportunity to use skills of which he is proud. Fifth, the district is not strapped for money and can afford to employ him in this capacity. Sixth, the district is experiencing declining enrollments and does not need to replace him. Finally, the Superintendent and Board of Education are anxious to get rid of the teacher but want to avoid controversy. The terms of the settlement are, therefore, reasonable from the vantage point of all parties and reflect the personal and situational circumstances which exist in the district.

The Monetary Value of Inducements

Even though the inducements contained in most settlements partially respond to the incompetent teacher's needs, the costs associated with these inducements rarely equal or approach the savings effected by the teacher's departure. Seven of the thirty teachers who were induced to leave received nothing in exchange for their 'voluntary' separation. One additional teacher received only the promise of good recommendations for non-teaching positions. The remaining teachers received inducements that cost the district money, but in only two of these cases did the settlement equal or exceed the savings realized by the district in the following year. Mr. Blum was paid what he would have received as a classroom teacher. The other teacher received a settlement that exceeded the costs of her replacement. This particular teacher received difference pay for one semester (the difference between what he would have earned as a teacher and the cost of his substitute), a $10,000 lump sum payment, a $7500 award for psychiatric treatment, and $4500 per year for four years to work as a consultant. By the end of the second year, however, this teacher's departure no longer cost the district money; the district was saving approximately $7500 annually.

Conclusion

In this chapter we have discussed the role of pressure, negotiations, unions and inducements in influencing incompetent teachers to submit a resignation or to request an early retirement. Given the limited financial value of the inducements offered by school districts, we are inclined to view inducements as playing only a supportive role in securing resignations and early retirements. Pressure, not inducements, is cast in the leading role. It convinces the union that the administration means business and has the evidence to prove its case.[8] Moreover, the pressure is a source of intense stress for the incompetent teacher and serves as a vivid reminder that dismissal is more than a remote possibility. A 'voluntary' separation offers welcome relief from the stressful situation and allows the teacher to save face (Goffman, 1955) by avoiding the stigma of dismissal. Under these circumstances, inducements simply tip the scales in favor of resignation by weakening the forces which bind the teacher to an unhappy marriage. Negotiations are the vehicle through which the administrator identifies the nature of these forces and discovers the means for diminishing their strength. If the teacher is worried about the eroding effects of inflation on his/her retirement income, the administrator can alleviate this fear somewhat by providing additional years of credited service towards retirement. If the teacher fears unemployment, the administrator can reduce the fear by promising to give favorable recommendations. The union assists the administration in closing the deal by counseling and persuading the teacher to leave quietly.

Notes

1 From a purely technical viewpoint, a school district does not dismiss temporary teachers; rather, it *declines to rehire* them. This latter action is functionally equivalent to dismissal.
2 This estimate is based on two assumptions. First, temporary teachers are dismissed (not rehired) and not given the opportunity to resign. Second, since tenured teachers comprise 80 per cent of the teaching force in California, we assumed that at least 80 per cent of the teachers who were induced to leave possessed tenure.
3 Fournier (1984) found in his study of Tennessee secondary school principals that they commonly used documentation to remove teachers from their teaching assignments. Coercion was also a common practice.
4 For example, Charles Bowen v. United States Postal Service *et al.*, 103 S.Ct. 588 (1983); Vaca v. Sipes, 386 U.S. 171 (1967); and Steele v. Louisville and Nashville Ry. Co., 323 U.S. 192 (1944).
5 Steele v. Louisville and Nashville Ry. Co., 323 U.S. 192 (1944).
6 Kutner (1984) in his study of teacher retirement in the state of California also found that health and income from consultancies affected the decision of teachers to retire early. He assumed that all of these teachers had resigned voluntarily. Our research indicates that some of these retirements are involuntary and provides insight into how and why these two factors affect the early retirement decision.
7 The research of Mitchell *et al.* (1981) on the poor performer also indicates that supervisors are more likely to be lenient with subordinates when they are perceived as trying and putting forth the effort to do the job.
8 The union owes its members the duty of fair representation. If the union becomes a silent ally of the administration without first establishing that the teacher is incompetent and is being treated fairly by the administration, the union would not in our judgment be fulfilling its duty of fair representation. We scrutinized each case in which there was information about the union's involvement to see if it had denied the teacher fair representation. In all but one of the cases where the union cooperated with the administration to induce the teacher to leave, there was ample documentation to support the charge of incompetence. In the one case which represented an exception, the President of the union visited the class of the teacher on two different occasions before agreeing to cooperate.

Chapter 5

Anatomy of Dismissal

In the preceding chapter we argued that administrators rarely dismiss a teacher for incompetence; they prefer to induce the poor performer to resign or to request early retirement. The reluctance of administrators to dismiss a tenured teacher for incompetence stems from multiple sources — the ambiguities inherent in teacher evaluation, the desires of administrators to avoid conflict and unpleasantness, the staff morale problems which are created unless the teacher is uniformly disliked by colleagues, and the laws governing dismissal. In this chapter the reader will acquire a fine-grained understanding of the dismissal process and further insight into why administrators are reluctant to use this ultimate sanction.

Before we explore the nature of a dismissal proceeding and the events which follow it, we want to underscore two points. First, we wish to remind the reader that administrators are inclined to remove only those teachers who are in a state of performance collapse. Their incompetence is generally multi-faceted and extensive. The teacher is unable to plan effectively, to present material clearly, to maintain discipline, and to promote the academic growth of pupils. Occasionally, the incompetence represents egregious failure but is much more limited in scope. In such cases, the poor performer is woefully deficient in only one facet of teaching, and this deficiency is usually discipline. Failure in classroom discipline seemingly is legitimate grounds for dismissal even when the students in the teacher's class are making satisfactory progress. The following excerpt from an appellate court judge underscores in vivid language the importance of this facet of teacher incompetence:

> The essence of the charge against Y was that he was unable to maintain an orderly classroom. . . . It is undisputed that Y's

students met the academic standards appropriate to measure the skill with which he imparted information relevant to the subjects he covered. We view as no less important than academic knowledge the teaching of standards of civilized behavior necessary to the functioning of society. Order and discipline should never be exalted to the detriment of learning or of the concepts basic to a free society, but neither should appropriate group behavior be discarded as irrelevant to the educational process. A school which produced well-educated sociopaths would be as inimical to democracy as one which created well-educated robots.

This teacher's discipline problems were obvious, persistent, and serious. They included students fighting, playing soccer in the classroom, yelling over the school intercom, wrestling, throwing pencils, using vulgar language, screaming at the teacher, and engaging in a tug-of-war over some tape.

Second, the reader should assume that the dismissal decision has been preceded by a salvage attempt, a 90-day notice of deficiency, an abortive effort to obtain an induced exit, and a notice of intent to dismiss. Since these steps have been discussed in earlier chapters, we will not repeat our descriptions of these administrative responses to teacher incompetence (Bridges, 1990).

The Dismissal Proceeding

Dismissal proceedings go through a number of phases and may be either public or private depending upon the preferences of the teacher. The most common phases include: discovery, direct examination, cross-examination, closing argument, and deliberation. Let us briefly examine each of these phases and consider some of the problems and issues which may arise.

Discovery

Prior to the hearing, the opposing parties may disclose information and evidence which they propose to use in the hearing. This disclosure prevents the type of 'trial by ambush' that is so familiar to Perry Mason fans. Discovery is designed to avoid surprises and to expedite the proceedings; it is usually mandated by state statute. During the discovery phase, the disctrict administration is generally obligated to present the oral and written evidence that will be used against the teacher. The oral segment of the process involves a question and answer session conducted by the teacher's defense counsel. This interrogation allows the defense counsel to assess the weight of the evidence against the teacher and to gauge the effectiveness of the administration in presenting the district's case. The defense counsel also obtains all information regarding the dates and times of incidents relevant to the charges, the names and addresses of potential witnesses, and copies of all related documentation. Failure to provide this information may be interpreted as a denial of the teacher's right to due process.

Direct examination

This is usually the first phase of the actual hearing. During this phase, the district administration seeks to establish that a pattern of incompetent performance exists despite efforts to assist the teacher in overcoming these deficiencies. The testimony of the school principal and documentation play an important role in this phase; in fact, they often represent the most significant element of the district's presentation. During this phase, the teacher's legal counsel may object to leading questions, that is, questions that provide the basis for the desired answer within the question. In addition, the teacher's defense counsel may object to answers that are based on hearsay, that attempt to go beyond the scope of the question, or that are unrelated to a specific charge.

To reduce the likelihood of being distracted or confused by these objections, the administrator must be thoroughly familiar with evidence and the testimony that need to be presented in support of each charge. The administrator is not solely dependent on his memory and ability to recall, however; he may refer to notes and documentation that he has prepared in connection with the teacher's dismissal.

Cross-examination

During this phase, the attorney for the teacher seeks to show that administrative bias, lack of support, and unfair treatment created conditions that made it virtually impossible for the teacher to succeed. In attempting to discredit the administration, the attorney will ask questions that are designed to establish one or more of the following (taken in large part from Evans; n.d.):

1 The administration created a teaching assignment that precluded success. For example, the teacher had too many unruly students, too many preparations, and a classroom that was

located in an area that was filled with noise and distractions.

2 Administrators failed to comply with established state laws and/or local board policies and related rules and regulations. For example, the principal failed to provide the teacher with a sufficiently specific statement of deficiencies.

3 The teacher's supervisors practiced 'unequal application of the law'. That is to say, the teacher was criticized for acts for which other teachers, acting in a similar manner, received no such criticism.

4 Administrators were biased against the teacher. The defense counsel will try to establish that 'philosophical' differences, not deficiencies in teaching skills, accounted for the teacher's difficulties.

5 The administration was punishing the teacher for exercising his right to free speech or to participate actively in the teachers' union.

6 Administrators did not give adequate support and guidance to the teacher. In other words, supervisor shortcomings account for the teacher's poor performance.

7 The administration 'harassed' the teacher through holding an excessive number of classroom observations and conferences. As a result, the teacher became overanxious and was unable to improve.

8 Administrators were remiss in not explicitly proscribing certain behavior for the teacher. For example, the principal stated, 'It would be helpful if . . .' and 'I would appreciate it if . . .' Such statements, according to the teacher's defense counsel, do not let the teacher know that the behavior is unacceptable and should be stopped.

9 The administration cannot prove that alleged written or oral communication with the teacher actually occurred. 'You never told me'.

10 The credibility of administrative testimony is suspect because the supervisor lacks subject matter expertise, teaching experience at the teacher's grade level, and experience in supervising and evaluating teachers.

11 The administrator's recollections of specific details are hazy and subject to confusion.

In addition to these specific approaches to cross-examination, the counsel for the respondent may

attempt to intimidate, rile, or lull the administrator
into certain reactions, comments, or emotional man-
ifestations which, in turn, may cause the members of
the hearing panel to speculate about the involved
administrator(s) composure, stability, and general
leadership ability. Such speculation can do nothing
but damage the district's case. (Evans, n.d.)

Closing argument

When both sides have presented their evidence, the attorneys for the
school district and the teacher make their final oral argument to the
adjudicator. Since the burden of proof rests on the school district,
the school attorney has the opportunity to speak first and last. After
the closing arguments have been presented, the adjudicator recesses the
hearing for the purpose of deliberation.

Deliberation

During this phase, the adjudicator reviews the evidence to determine
whether there is cause (in this instance, the cause is incompetence) for
the proposed dismissal action and whether any of the teacher's substantive and procedural rights have been violated. As we have stated
on several occasions, the teacher does not have to prove that he is
competent; rather, the district must prove that the teacher is incompetent. In judging whether the district has proved that the teacher is
incompetent, the adjudicator considers the greater weight of all the
evidence, not the number of witnesses or exhibits.

The testimony of one witness may be more persuasive than
that of ten, because opportunity for knowledge, information
possessed, and manner of testifying determine the weight to be
given to the testimony. (Phay, 1982)

After reviewing the evidence presented by both sides, the adjudicator issues its decision. The written decision ordinarily contains
findings of facts, a determination of the issues, and an order; if one of
the adjudicators disagrees, the decision may also include a dissent. To
clarify further these various components of a written decision, let us
consider a few examples.

In the judgment of the adjudicator, the district may or may not
have successfully substantiated its charges against the teacher. The
findings of fact in the written decision reflect the adjudicator's judg-

ment on these matters. For example, the Commission of Professional Competence ruled in No. L-26607 (November 15, 1982) that the Los Angeles City Unified School District established 38 of the facts it presented in its case; each of these facts is numbered and described in the decision. Two such facts are reproduced below:

XI

It is true that on or about November 28, 1979, some parents of students in Mr R's class complained to Mrs B. (the principal) that Mr R. was spending more time giving 'courtesy lectures' than he was teaching, and that, consequently, the children were being deprived of instruction. In going over her records, Mrs B. noted that the greater part of the instructional time in Mr R's Period 6 class had been spent in 'courtesy lectures', in that there were eight days of 'courtesy lectures' and 15 days of actual electronics instruction between October 22 and November 26, 1979. The above situation was communicated to the respondent as Mrs B. directed Mr R. to cease giving 'courtesy lectures' and to resume teaching electronics and to use the school resources to improve class discipline.

XII

It is true that on or about December 14, 1979, Mrs B. visited Mr R's Period 5 Advanced Electronics class. She observed that he failed to properly prepare for instruction to students, in that he did not provide for equipment he believed to be necessary for the students. The students were making salt and pepper shakers. When Mrs B. asked why the students were engaged in an activity inappropriate for an Advanced Electronics class, Mr R. stated that he needed some breathing time. The above project was not authorized for that period Electronics class; and though it was better than delivering 'courtesy lectures', it was not a substantial curriculum activity.

The Commission also ruled that the district failed to establish two of the facts; one of these follows:

While it is true that on or about January 25, 1980, Mr B. (assistant principal) found two students from Mr R's class wandering about the PE field, and Mr R. stated he had sent them out of the room for misbehavior; he followed normal procedure, and it was not established that respondent was responsible for their failure to return to class.

Following the finding of facts, the adjudicator ordinarily determines the issues, i.e., concludes whether cause for dismissal exists. In the case that we have just been discussing, the Commission on Professional Competence stated:

> Pursuant to the foregoing findings of fact, the Commission makes the following determination of issues:
>
> > Cause for dismissal of respondent exists pursuant to Education Code Section 44932 (d) in that he has demonstrated incompetency, by reason of each of Findings III through XXXX, and XXXXIII, and all of them.

The final component of the decision ordinarily consists of the order or disposition of the case. The order in the above case is reproduced below:

> The following order is hereby made:
>
> > The respondent, Mr R., should be and he hereby is dismissed as a permanent certificated employee of the Los Angeles City Unified School District.

Since all three members of the Commission on Professional Competence concurred in the decision, there was no dissent. If one of the members had dissented, he could have included his dissent in the decision.

When a Commission member decides to include a dissenting opinion, his dissent may relate to the findings of fact, the determination of issues, the order, or all three. Moreover, the dissenter may or may not choose to offer reasons for his disagreement with the decision. To illustrate how extensive a dissent may be, we have included a few excerpts from a five-page, single-spaced dissent; this particular dissent offers reasons for objecting to all three components of the decision and makes strong statements on behalf of the teacher:

> *In regard to finding of fact IX on page 9* (alleged lack of academic achievement by the respondent's pupils), the respondent's

pupil failure rate is not significant or indicative of the respondent's professional competence. The respondent's pupil failure rate is reasonable in light of the District-wide pupil failure rate, shown by exhibits and testimony to range from 92 per cent to 20 per cent (8 per cent to 80 per cent passage rate). Mr M. (department chair) testified that the reason for this variation was under investigation and unknown. The respondent's pupil failure rate is approximately central to the District range of failure rates and therefore the respondent's performance must be considered typical of District teachers of similar courses.... It was not established that the pupil failure rates were atypical or related to the respondent's professional performance; they were, in fact, remarkably low in view of the fact that the respondent was teaching students who had persistently failed mathematics prior to entry into high school.

In regard to Determination of Issues III, incompetence has not been demonstrated and dissent in regard to the Findings listed is offered as proof. Furthermore, the Findings offered by the Commission do not prove any significant lack of knowledge of subject matter or failure as a mediator of learning and therefore would not support a charge of incompetence.

In regard to the Order, the respondent is an ordinarily competent teacher of basic mathematics, and typical of teachers of this subject. His education in counseling and psychology and his strength as a disciplinarian and counselor suggest that he may, in fact, be significantly more able than most since the problem of the basic math teacher lies more with discipline and motivation than with mediation of learning. It should be recognized that the respondent's pupils have had some eight years of (presumably excellent) instruction in mathematics, with little or no effect, before coming to him. There is no reason to dismiss this man, and the District will not find a better man to replace him.

The dissenter in this case was the Commission member chosen by the teacher.

Dismissal and its Aftermath

The District Loses

When school districts attempt to dismiss teachers for incompetence, success is by no means a foregone conclusion. As we pointed out in Chapter 2, the Commission on Professional Competence overturned thirty-eight of the ninety-one dismissal decisions made by local school districts during the three-year period 1978–80. The data on success rates that we have been able to compile from other sources (Gold and others, 1978; Thurston, 1981; and Shafer, 1987) reveal a similar pattern. In these three studies the dismissal decisions of local school districts were upheld approximately 60 per cent of the time. Their decisions were sustained in 130 of 211 cases and overturned in eighty-one instances. Inexplicably, the success rates varied dramatically from one state to another — 37 per cent in Illinois (Thurston, 1981) to 77 per cent in Nebraska (Shafer, 1987).

If an adjudicator reverses a dismissal decision, school officials must reinstate the teacher and cope with the aftermath of reinstatment. When terminated teachers return to their former employers, the results are generally dismal from the district's point of view. Most of the teachers who are rated poor at the time of termination are also rated poor after reinstatement (Gold and others, 1978). The same difficulties that originally led to termination recur in the vast majority of cases. Moreover, reversals subsequently produce a bad atmosphere between labor and management and additional problems at the bargaining table. Reversal rarely stimulates contract and procedural changes which aim to avoid future problems. These negative results coincide with those found in studies of reinstatement in the private sector (Jones, 1961; McDermott and Newhams, 1971; and Malinowski, 1981).

Faced with these unwelcome prospects, an unswerving commitment to quality education, or perhaps an intense desire to win or to make a point, some districts will continue to pursue the issue. In the words of Yogi Berra, the former manager of the New York Yankees, 'It ain't over 'til it's over'.

The Bayview District (the hypothetical name for the district involved in this case) illustrates the Yogiism. In 1978, Bayview was a small, crowded school district known for its low test scores, low-income families and large numbers of non-English-speaking students. Ten years later, test scores are up and discipline problems are down; it is one of the few districts nationwide to have had three schools commended for excellence by the United States Department of Education.

A new superintendent engineered the turnaround. He initiated strict accountability, tough discipline, and higher expectations for students and staff. Higher expectations for teachers translated into numerous teacher dismissals. For his efforts, the superintendent was viewed by some as a forceful educational leader and by others as a tyrant. Supporters and opponents alike agreed on one thing; the superintendent was a determined man.

Nowhere does his determination reveal itself more than in teacher evaluation and his treatment of those teachers who fail to meet the district's high expectations for performance. The following case shows his determination and gives meaning to the statement, 'If at first you don't succeed, try, try again'. After reading the case, there understandably will be those who will ask, 'Is justice being served? For whom?'

In May, 1982, the superintendent served Mr X with an Accusation and Statement of Charges and sought to dismiss him. According to the superintendent, dismissal was warranted on three grounds: incompetency, evident unfitness for service, and persistent violation of regulations. Nearly one year later the Commission on Professional Compentence issued its decision. It ruled that there was no factual basis for the accusations of incompetency and unfitness for service but determined that the teacher persistently violated the reasonable regulations of the District's board of education. These violations took the following forms:

B Too often students received the same study assignment even though their proficiencies and skills varied in different subject matters. And although there were periodic attempts at correcting the same by Mr X, nevertheless there continued inadequate individualization of instruction. Rather than group the students according to their abilities to learn a particular lesson — not always but too many times — all students, regardless of their abilities, received the same assignment.

C There was a lack of classroom disciplinary control and therefore a lack of learning environment in respondent's classes

— as evidenced by students wandering about the room, playing, joking, copying the lesson assignments of others; by sometimes loud talking and at other times a constant undertone of talking and chatting; — plus a lack of attentiveness by the students to Mr X. Respondent was, at times, unmindful of these events occurring in the classroom. Further, the disciplinary techniques suggested to the respondent by the District to control such situations were not always used and when used were not always used effectively.

D   And, too often too many students were not 'on task'; that is, the students were not performing the lesson then currently assigned. While it is to be expected, especially in the primary grades, that not all students will be on task at all times, nevertheless such a failure was unusually prevalent and persistent in respondent's classroom. Such a deficiency was not prevalent, however, during split reading classes or small-group instruction.

E   Then too, there were several classroom observations in which it was noted that respondent's instructions to the children were not clear. This caused these students either not to undertake the assignment or to consult among themselves as to that which was being required of them.

F   Despite repeated and specific instructions to do so, respondent on several occasions failed to submit his classroom lesson plans to the principal and to timely communicate with the principal concerning such plans.

H   There was no evidence of respondent's willful refusal to correct the above deficiencies.

The inadequacies of respondent's performance, as documented in the immediate preceding finding, were well documented through classroom observations made by the principal, but also made by other staff as well ... So also, during this time, these and other deficiencies were brought to respondent's attention with regularity through specific and summary written evaluations, personal conferences and other modes of possible assistance.

Although the Commission found that these deficiencies existed, it ruled by a 2 to 1 vote that the Accusation and Statement of Charges, not the teacher, should be dismissed.

The superintendent and the district decided to pursue the issue. They appealed the decision in the Superior Court of California but lost again. Shortly thereafter, the district took its case against Mr X to a third arena — the state committee that oversees teacher credentials. After reviewing the case, the committee refused to consider it. While awaiting the decision of this committee, the district issued another 90-day notice of deficiency to Mr X, a notice that could lead to a new attempt to fire him.

After winning three legal battles against the district, spending most of the year on sick leave due to stress, and facing another possible effort to dismiss him, Mr X agreed to accept $20,800 in return for his resignation. According to Mr X's attorney,

> It became very clear some time ago that the district was not going to turn around. I think he just got to the end of his rope. It can really take it out of you, any kind of litigation, but especially when it's involved with your life's work. I think the hardest part of this for Mr X was he loves teaching and he loves those kids.

The District Wins

If the adjudicator orders the dismissal of the teacher, the joy and jubilation of district officials may be short-lived. The dismissed teacher, like the district, has the legal right to contest the decision. Yogi Berra's immortal words are worth repeating, 'It ain't over 'til it's over'.

To understand once again the aptness of Yogi's famous line, let us review the case of Mr Y who was dismissed for incompetence in 1982. For nearly a decade he has battled in the courts to be reinstated to his former position. He has taken his case to the State Supreme

Court on three different occasions and to the United States Supreme Court twice. Each time he bases his claim on a different legal theory. These legal theories fall into three major categories: wrongful discharge, deprivation of constitutional rights, and discrimination. He wants his job back, damages for emotional distress, and lost wages for the period that he has been out of work. The chronology of events surrounding his dismissal is reproduced below. These events speak for themselves.

CHRONOLOGY OF EVENTS

January, 1982:

Superintendent notifies Y of specified acts of incompetency; appends two previous formal evaluations and a copy of letter dated April, 1981 notifying him of specified acts of incompetency.

June, 1982:

Superintendent files notice of accusation and alleges cause for dismissal because of Y's failure to maintain a suitable learning environment in his junior high school classroom. Teacher requests a hearing before the Commission on Professional Competence.

November, 1982:

Commission on Professional Competence issues a two-to-one decision concluding that Y is incompetent to teach and orders his dismissal. Commission also finds Y guilty of two instances of false testimony.

December, 1982:

Y seeks review of his dismissal in the Superior Court of the State on the grounds that his dismissal violated due process of law.

June, 1983:

Superior Court, in an independent review, finds that (1) cause for dismissal had been established; (2) each of the notices and evaluations complied with statutory requirements; and (3) Y's alteration of his testimony before the Commission on Professional Competence constituted unclean hands.

November, 1984:

Y seeks damages ($100,000 each from members of Board of Education and three school administrators) in the Superior

Court for breach of contract and conspiracy to defraud. [Referred to hereafter as the Common Law action.]

March, 1985:

Y seeks damages and relief for violations of his civil and constitutional rights under 42 USC 1983; for violations of his federal and state constitutional guarantees of free speech, due process, and equal protection; and for violations of the State Fair Employment Practices Act. [Referred to hereafter as the Civil Rights action.] Filed in State Superior Court.

June, 1985:

The State Court of Appeals upholds the June, 1983, judgment of the Superior Court. Applies the substantial evidence standard of review and concludes that there was sufficient evidence to support the Superior Court's decision that 'in the aggregate, the events and facts constitute cause for the dismissal of Y'.

July, 1985:

The State Court of Appeals denies Y's petition for rehearing the June, 1985 decision.

August 1, 1985:

Y appeals to State Supreme Court.

August, 1985:

State Supreme Court denies Y's request for a hearing on the July, 1985 ruling of the state Court of Appeals.

September, 1985:

Y files demur in Superior Court on Civil Rights action.

September, 1985:

Y amends November, 1984 Common Law action. Seeks damages for Wrongful Discharge, Conspiracy to Defraud, Intentional Infliction of Emotional Distress, and Negligent Infliction of Emotional Distress.

November, 1985:

Y takes his claim to the United States District Court. He alleges that the school district violated his rights under the fourteenth amendment of the United States Constitution and 42 USC. Sections 1981 and 1983 by terminating his employment on account of his ethnic origin. Y requests compensatory damages for lost wages and mental distress as well as punitive damages.

November, 1985:

Y seeks a writ of certiorari from the United States Supreme

Court to review the decision of the State Court of Appeals (June, 1985 judgment) on the grounds that his dismissal violated the due process clause of the fourteenth amendment to the United States Constitution.

January, 1986:

US Supreme Court denies the writ of certiorari requested by Y in November, 1985.

January, 1987:

US Federal District Court rules that Y's action (dated November, 1985) was barred by his prior unsuccessful litigation against the school district in the state court.

December, 1987:

Y consolidates the Common Law action and the Civil Rights action brought to the State Superior Court in November, 1984, and March, 1985.

February, 1988:

The Federal Court of Appeals for the Ninth Circuit affirms the Federal District Court's January, 1987 finding.

June, 1988:

The US Supreme Court denies Y's writ of certiorari in the matter decided by the Federal Court of Appeals on February, 1988.

March, 1989:

State Superior Court dismisses the Common Law and Civil Rights actions.

May, 1989:

Y appeals the March, 1989 ruling of the State Superior Court to the State Court of Appeals.

July, 1990:

State Appeals Court affirms March, 1989 judgment of Superior Court.

August, 1990:

Y petitions Appeals Court for rehearing.

August, 1990:

Appeals Court denies request for rehearing.

August, 1990:

Petitions State Supreme Court to review July and August 1990, decisions of Appeals Court; decision pending.

Despite these numerous court appearances and legal reversals, Mr Y continues his quest for reinstatement. His deep sense of being wronged is reflected in the following letter (dated June, 1990) to me:

Dear Dr. Bridges:

It has been reported that I am the only tenured teacher in the entire state who has been fired on the false allegation of 'incompetence'. The Courts have determined that the School District failed to comply with State Law. This has in effect abolished teacher tenure in the State and rendered permanent employment contracts void.... Assistance is needed to get my 'day in court' to show that my discharge was wrong. All that are needed are your signature and your qualifications on the enclosed application....

... I have tried for eight years to have my day in court to restore my life damaged by the malicious and ruinous accusation of 'incompetence.'

... I believe it is the duty and obligation of the justice system to rectify violations occurring in the enforcement of our laws. It has become open season for intimidations and harassment in the workplace; and our schools and America's productivity stagnate in mediocrity. School Districts must be held accountable to our laws and Constitutions, and we must continually work toward excellence for our schools and for America.

Thank you for your kind attention.

Sincerely yours,

Mr Y.

The reactions of the Superintendent to Mr Y's continued legal efforts sum up the opinions of many administrators on the dismissal process:

Dear Dr. Bridges:

... Dismissing a tenured teacher in this state is not a process — it currently is a career. ... a most trying procedure.

Sincerely,

Mr S.

(letter to the author dated August, 1990)

How typical is Mr Y's case? We simply do not know. Data on the frequency of appeals are limited. In the one state (Nebraska) for which we have data, twenty-six (roughly one third) of the seventy-eight teachers whose dismissals were upheld appealed the decision. These cases span the period from 1984 to 1987 (Shafer, 1987). We have no idea how many times these teachers chose to bite the apple. Depending upon their resources and their resolve, they, like Mr Y, may litigate their perceived injustices until one or both are exhausted.

Summary and Conclusion

In this chapter we focused on the events which follow a district's decision to dismiss a tenured teacher for incompetence. We described the five phases of a dismissal proceeding — discovery, direct examination, cross-examination, closing argument, and deliberation — and identified where administrators may encounter trouble. We also discussed what can happen when a district wins or loses at the dismissal proceeding. Neither of the cases which we examined is typical; rather, both represent the extremes to which either party to the dismissal proceeding may go under the present legal system if there is the determination to 'win' at all costs.

We now understand why dismissal may be referred to by some writers as the corporate equivalent of the death penalty. Dismissal is an ordeal for teachers; they can sit on death row for years while pursuing a reversal. Even when they win, it may be a hollow victory. The district may decide to press its case and, like the fabled TV detective, Columbo, hound the suspect until he crumbles under the pressure. Districts, on the other hand, face equally unpleasant prospects. The teacher, like the accused criminal, is presumed to be innocent until proven guilty. Proving incompetence in a dismissal proceeding, as we have shown, is not straightforward and similarly represents an ordeal for administrators. Even if the district's decision is sustained, the teacher, using different legal theories, may contest the decision in various legal forums. Where dismissal is concerned, 'It ain't over 'til it's over'. Viewed in this light, the sparing use of dismissal is understandable.

If the dismissal process is a seemingly endless ordeal for administrators and teachers, how is the process viewed by those who sit in judgment? Although the evidence bearing on this question is limited, it is unequivocal. The following poem written by a career teacher while serving one full year on a dismissal hearing panel (a three-member Commission on Professional Competence) sums up his views on the process:

AND PAUL THOUGHT *HE* HAD SOMETHING TO CRY ABOUT

Listen all parents and please give ear
To the terrible tale you're about to hear:
From **June, 78** to **June, 79**,
It was my misfortune to be assigned
To a three-man panel whose job would be
Determining a teacher's competency.

The Super said, 'What a break for you:
To hear a teacher dismissal case through.
It can only last a week or two'.
So I jumped at the chance and landed in place
Beside the Judge in charge of the case ...

The charges numbered ninety four:
From Lateness (persistent), Preparation (Poor)
To Contempt for every Administrator
Who she felt could not add two and two,
And certainly couldn't tell *her* what to do.

So on and on the travesty went
To the tune of $200,000 spent
And 3,000 hours, and 200 days
While I sat thinking of different ways
To convey to parents and payers of tax
How incredibly wasteful, stupid, and lax
Are the laws that protect such classroom hacks.

So born of that District Hearing room
I penned these words presaging doom.
In this hour of darkness and need of truth,
You parents must waken and listen to hear
This cry more crucial to your country's youth
Than any wild ride of Paul Revere.

James Van Wagoner[1]

The dismissal process as portrayed in this chapter is patently imperfect and in need of major repair.[2] The opponents of tenure, fueled by our 'terrible tale', will demand radical surgery. They will assert, 'Tenure is the villain. Abolish it, and the ills will disappear'.

Perhaps, but most certainly the abuses of a by-gone era will reappear. Prior to the enactment of state tenure laws, teachers served at the pleasure of school boards. Teachers could be dismissed for good cause, bad cause, or no cause at all. With their authority and power to dismiss unchecked, some boards engaged in a variety of questionable practices. Teachers were dismissed because of political reasons and because board members desired to make places for friends and relatives, to save money by diminishing the number of teachers, to lower costs by creating vacancies to be filled by inexperienced teachers, and to punish those who were 'disloyal' to the administration (Lebeis, 1939; NEA, 1924). Such practices stimulated state and national teacher associations to press for tenure legislation; by 1980 nearly every state had adopted statewide tenure (Stelzer and Banthin 1980).

Less drastic alternatives than the abolition of tenure are warranted. In creating and assessing these alternatives, policy makers should strive to balance the interests of students in a quality education against the interests of teachers in continued employment. The current system of tenure and the process for revoking it do not. The scales are tipped in favor of teachers, not students. In the final chapter we propose several changes in the tenure system and the dismissal process which will restore this balance. We believe that these changes will also repair many of the defects described in this chapter.

Notes

1 After I received this poem from its author, I asked him to clarify several of the factual issues which he referred to in his poem. His reply was as follows:

Dear Professor Bridges:
      In response to your questions, I checked my files and found the hearing did indeed last from June to June. I was selected by the respondent's school district (not mine) as their representative on the panel which consisted of an Administrative Law Judge, a teacher selected by the Teacher's Organization of the respondent's school, and myself. Although the Hearing *lasted* through a full year, the panel did not meet every day. Periodically, for various reasons, the Hearing would be 'continued to' and we would have breaks of one to two weeks or even a month before we took it up again. I *was* on the panel for a full year, but the panel did not meet every day of every week. When it did meet, I was assigned full-time, and the daily time served varied from five to seven hours. The weeks of actual Hearing time would be about eighteen

plus an additional two for discussion and decision making. If you take five days per week, you get a total of 100 days served by each panelist involved (excluding the Judge), or a total of 200 days. In this stanza, I'm trying to convey the *total* amount of time and money wasted. The 3000 hours includes the time of the various witnesses plus the three administrators who were in attendance every day of the Hearing. Since I began the stanza with $200,000, (It was actually closer to $250,000, but who's counting?), I assumed, perhaps naively, that the reader would conclude the 3000 hours and 200 days were also totals.

Sincerely,

James Van Wagoner (real name, used with permission of the author)

2 For a somewhat different view of the dismissal process, see Gross (1988). He analyzed case decisions in New York State in which tenured teachers were charged with incompetence or conduct unbecoming a professional. He too finds the system imperfect but concentrates his analysis and suggested reforms on the meaning and measurement of good teaching and the criteria for evaluating teacher conduct and performance. Moreover, Gross maintains that the disciplinary system is unfair to teachers. In the ten year period which he studied (1977–1987), he reports only twenty cases in New York state involving the dismissal of a tenured teacher for incompetence. He never raises a question about why there are so few cases and what the implications might be for students. The lack of proper standards for judging the competence of teachers deters administrators from dealing forthrightly with poor performers in the classroom and is far more injurious to students than to teachers. Unfortunately, the students who are most likely to be harmed are the students who need a quality education the most — the disadvantaged. See my discussion of this issue in the last chapter where I highlight the irony in the 14th Amendment — due process for teachers and unequal protection for students, especially minorities.

Chapter 6

Managing the Poor Performer: A Case

Thus far, we have examined the various ways in which administrators respond to the incompetent teacher and the factors which shape these responses. We have argued that administrators are unlikely to confront the poor performers in their midst unless one or more of the following conditions prevail: (i) the district attaches high importance to teacher evaluation; (ii) the district is relatively small and is faced with parental complaints and/or declining enrollments; and (iii) the district is experiencing a financial squeeze and is faced with parental complaints and/or declining enrollments. Under these conditions, administrators are likely to criticize teachers for their poor performance, to launch salvage attempts, and to press for induced resignations or early retirement rather than dismissal if the teacher fails to improve. In the absence of these conditions, administrators, like their counterparts in business and other more prestigious professions, are inclined to tolerate and protect the poor performer.

To illustrate how these conditions affect the responses of administrators to incompetent teachers, the experiences of one California school district are described in this chapter. The case is a provocative example of the ideas discussed in chapters 2, 3 and 4. It vividly shows how one school district chose to deal with the problem of teacher incompetence in a period of retrenchment. This particular district fell on hard times in the late 1970s and was forced to prune its staff. The reduction occurred on the basis of performance, not seniority. Although parents played a key role in initiating this personnel policy, the administration exerted considerable influence on how the policy was actually implemented. Over a period of several years, the administration induced a rather large proportion of its teaching staff to submit resignations or to request early retirements. These teachers were the weakest ones working in the district.

The Context

Ocean View (a pseudonym) is a small residential community nestled in the foothills south of Los Angeles. Most of the homes afford sweeping views of the Pacific Ocean and the extraordinary thirty-mile beach that forms the westernmost boundary of the town. Residents are fiercely proud of their smog-free environment and are staunch proponents of a slow-growth policy. They moved to Ocean View to escape the smog and the traffic congestion of Los Angeles and are determined to keep these urban ills out of their idyllic setting.

The Residents

The 7000 people who live in this community are relatively affluent. Most of the residents are employed in managerial and professional occupations and commute daily to Los Angeles. Women play rather traditional roles in their families and confine their outside activities to the League of Women Voters, local charities, churches and the schools which their children attend. The vast majority of households report annual incomes in excess of $70,000; only a handful of residents are receiving welfare payments from the government. People drive expensive cars, wear fashionable clothes, and live in high priced homes. They are college educated and expect their children to follow in their academic footsteps. By any indicator of social class, Ocean View residents belong to the upper-middle class.

The School District

The Ocean View Elementary School District currently operates two elementary schools (kindergarten through grade 5) and one middle school (grades 6–8). Each of the three schools has its own principal who reports directly to the Superintendent. The Ocean View Board of Education consists of five people who are chosen in a non-partisan election by the local voters. When Ocean View students are ready to enter high school, they attend the school in nearby Hillcrest. This high school offers a strong college preparatory program and is highly regarded by the admissions officers of the most prestigious universities on the west coast.

The Teachers' Union

Teachers in the Ocean View Elementary School District are affiliated with the California Teachers' Association.[1] In 1978 they negotiated a multi-year collective bargaining agreement with the local Board of Education. This agreement remains in effect and although it encompasses a broad spectrum of items, it does not create a.straitjacket for the administration. For example, in the area of personnel evaluation, the union has chosen to impose few constraints on administrators. The agreement stipulates that unannounced, as well as scheduled, observations may be used in the evaluation process. It also allows parent and student comments to be used in the evaluation of teachers if the administration deems these comments to be sufficiently reliable and valid. The agreement does not specify the criteria for evaluating teachers; this crucial decision is left to the discretion of the administration. The only noteworthy limitations cover the teacher's right to a conference, a copy of the evaluation, and recommendations for improvement if this is necessary.

The Financial Squeeze

Historically, Ocean View residents have exhibited strong support for their schools. As long as local property taxes were the major source of revenues, the school district ended each fiscal year with a hefty reserve — roughly $500,000 out of a total operating budget of $2.25 million dollars. However, when the state system for financing public education was altered in the 1970s, financial pressures began to mount. A crisis was precipitated in 1978 by the passage of Proposition 13. From 1978–79 to 1983–84, the total operating budget shrunk by more than $50,000 even though inflation was raging during most of this time period. Moreover the budgetary reserve dropped from a high of $618,973 in 1975 to a low of $64,000 in 1981–82. In this kind of fiscal environment, school officials could ill afford to create escape hatches for incompetent teachers and to keep teachers on the payroll when enrollments started to decline.

Declining Enrollments

Until 1978 the enrollments in the Ocean View Elementary School District were relatively stable. Enrollments fluctuated between 892

–918 students. Beginning in 1978, enrollments began to fall. By 1983 the enrollments had dropped to 689 students, a decline of nearly 25 per cent. To keep pace with the declines in student enrollment, the size of the district teaching staff was reduced from forty-five to thirty-six FTEs (full-time equivalents). In a period of four years, the district administration eliminated nine teaching positions due to declining enrollments. Although these actions affected only a few teachers in an absolute sense, these teachers accounted for a sizeable proportion of the district's total teaching staff.

The Response and the Reaction

Faced with declining enrollments and an impending budget crunch, the Ocean View administration decided to release some of its teachers. In accordance with state law, the administration issued notices of its intention to lay off the two teachers with the least seniority in the district. The names of these two teachers appeared in the *Ocean View Herald*, the local newspaper, in a weekly column written by the Superintendent of Schools. His article painted a dismal picture of school enrollments and finances and lamented the need to lay off these two teachers.

On the day following the publication of his column, the Superintendent received a phone call from a group of concerned parents. These parents asked to meet with him later that day to discuss the layoffs which he had announced. At the meeting, the five parents demanded to know why two of the finest teachers in the district were being released and the worst teachers were being retained. The Superintendent patiently explained the state law governing staff reductions and indicated that his hands were tied. One of the parents countered the Superintendent's explanation with this impassioned comment, 'Why don't you dismiss two teachers instead of laying off the cream of the crop? You know, as well as we do, that there are ineffective teachers in our district. They are the ones who should be leaving'. In response the Superintendent acknowledged the merit of their view but indicated that it was impractical. He summed up his position as follows, 'Dismissal is simply too costly, and you can never be sure of winning your case'. At that point, the parents asked for time to think about what he had said. They agreed to meet again on Monday of the following week.

When Monday morning arrived, the Superintendent held his scheduled meeting with these parents. As the conversation unfolded, it became evident that these parents had been busy over the weekend. They came armed with a bold proposal and the money to implement it. The spokesperson for the group described the plan and the events leading to it as follows:

> Over the weekend we created an educational foundation. We sent out an SOS (Save Our Schools) to the people in this community who care deeply about their schools. They contributed nearly $100,000 to ensure that their children receive a quality education. This money is to underwrite the legal costs associated with dismissing those teachers who are doing a poor job in the classroom. If this isn't enough money, we can raise more. We want to save the good teachers by getting rid of the bad ones.

Somewhat startled by what he had heard, the Superintendent said, 'I need to discuss your proposal with the Board. Let's get together two weeks from today, and I'll let you know their answer'.

At a special closed-session with the Board, the Superintendent described the proposal that he had received from the group of concerned parents. Although the Board was sympathetic to the sentiments underlying the proposal, it was extremely reluctant to dismiss teachers on the grounds of incompetence. A neighboring district had attempted to dismiss an ineffective teacher several years ago, and the case was still in litigation. The dismissal had divided the community, and the conflict was still not fully resolved.

After a lengthy discussion of the proposal and its ramifications, the Board and Superintendent finally reached agreement on their response. The Superintendent would meet with the group of concerned parents and would make a counterproposal on behalf of the Board. This counterproposal contained the following elements:

1 The administration will not lay off any teachers.
2 The administration will implement a rigorous program for evaluating teachers in the district.
3 The administration will make a concerted effort to help teachers improve if they are judged unsatisfactory.
4 The administration will force those teachers who fail to show substantial improvement to resign or to retire early.
5 The administration will assist these teachers in making the transition to retirement or to alternate forms of employment.
6 The SOS Foundation will provide the funds needed to implement the proposal over the next five years.

When the Superintendent met with the concerned parents, he explained why the Board was reluctant to use dismissal as a way of reducing the size of the staff and outlined what he and the Broad proposed to do instead. At first the group appeared lukewarm toward the proposal. However, as the Superintendent described how the proposal would be implemented, the group became convinced that the administration intended to deal forthrightly and responsibly with the problems of staff reduction and teacher quality. This conviction prompted the group to accept the Board's counterproposal.

The Plan and its Implementation

To fulfill its commitment to the SOS Foundation, the Board and the Superintendent instituted an integrated, comprehensive approach to teacher evaluation. The major features of this approach were as follows: (i) using management by objectives (MBO) to evaluate teachers; (ii) using multiple sources of information to determine how well teachers were performing in the classroom; (iii) providing principals with the resources to carry out their responsibility for improving instruction and getting rid of the poor performers; and (iv) holding principals account-able for evaluating and dealing with unsatisfactory teachers.

Management-by-Objectives

In the fall of each school year, the Principal meets with each teacher to complete an evaluation form. This form is organized around the state-mandated criteria for teacher evaluation: (a) standards of expected achievement for the teacher's students; (b) appropriate instructional techniques and strategies; (c) adherence to curricular objectives; (d) establishment and maintenance of a suitable learning environment; and (e) performance of non-classroom teaching duties. For each of these criteria, the Principal and the teacher construct a set of objectives, specify what actions will be taken to achieve the objectives, and identify how accomplishment will be determined.[2]

During the spring the Principal holds another conference with each teacher to review his or her progress in reaching the objectives. The Principal prepares a written report which summarizes the evidence that bears on the teacher's performance, sets targets for the following year, and indicates the assistance which the teacher will be given to reach these targets. Generally there are few surprises in this conference because the Principal frequently confers with teachers throughout the year about their progress in meeting the objectives which were established in the fall.

The Board and the Superintendent grant principals wide latitude in setting objectives and in deciding what indicators will be used to determine whether a teacher has met a particular criterion. Two of the principals handle these issues on an *ad hoc* basis. The third principal has provided the teaching staff with a copy of her philosophy and the sorts of things she looks for when conducting a classroom observation. She, like her fellow principals, targets objectives to those aspects of the teacher's performance which in her judgment show the greatest need for improvement.

Multiple Sources of Information

In judging how well teachers are performing in the classroom, principals are expected to use the following sources of information: (a) supervisory observations; (b) follow-up surveys; (c) needs assessments; and (d) parent comments. If the fall evaluation calls for other types of information to be used in assessing the accomplishment of the teacher's annual objectives, these sources are also included.

Supervisory observations

These observations are a critical component of the teacher evaluation program just as they are in other school districts. However, in Ocean View principals are required to spend from 20 to 30 per cent of the school day in classrooms observing their teachers. This activity is an integral part of the evaluation and of the principal's job. These observations are often unannounced, sometimes scheduled in advance, and occasionally requested by the teacher. Observations generally encompass an entire lesson from start to finish and are often followed by a conference, a written report, or both. If the follow-up is in writing, it usually describes what was happening in the classroom at the time of observation. The observer also offers candid assessments, relates his/her criticisms to the teacher's objectives, and suggests changes if these are deemed appropriate. The observation may also serve as an occasion for the principal to introduce other sources of information that bear on the teacher's performance. These features of the observation reports in Ocean View are exemplified in the following document:

OBSERVATION REPORT

OBSERVATION: Russ Brown, Math Teacher (7–8th grade)
OBSERVER: J. Jones, Principal
DATE: Monday ... April

This was an unscheduled observation.

Classroom Environment

No change in the same stimulating room environment that I always observe. A beautiful room filled with models, articles, and picture displays.

Classroom Control

No evidence of any problems.

The Lesson

Class started with a review of the problems on page 215 of the algebra text. Russ worked out several problems on the board and asked if there were any questions. There were none. Russ then announced a quiz for Friday and students started to work on their assignments. Four boys completed the day's assignment in 10 minutes and sat around the rest of the period. Another student who had not finished his assignment joined this group to discuss the game of Dungeons and Dragons.

Russ, why don't you have selected students work examples on the board by having them tell you what to do? By having students work examples on the board, you are going to find out at what point they don't understand a concept. This would in my opinion:

1 create an atmosphere that says you are interested in finding out at what point they don't understand the material and that you will work on it together;

2 create a little anxiety — which has proven to be a powerful motivator by putting students, momentarily, on the spot.

Do students still correct their own assignments? If so, how do you know when they really don't understand a concept?

Summary

What I saw today raises the same old questions/concerns:

1   At what point do you know when a student or a class understands or doesn't understand a concept? (My best guess would be not until you gave them a test on Friday.)
2   Why were these boys allowed to sit and converse? Why weren't they involved in some kind of math related activity? In your objectives, you stated that you would maintain a classroom atmosphere that allows students to pursue activities related to the math program when assigned work is completed (for example, games, topography, puzzles, manipulative devices, projects). This is not going to happen without direction from you.

I'm concerned for a number of reasons that go beyond what I observed during this lesson. Since this observation, I've done some follow up work at Hillcrest High School on last year's eighth graders recommended for the honors algebra program. Here are some facts you should be aware of:

There were ninety-six freshman students from all feeder schools enrolled in the honors algebra course at the beginning of this school year. This was enough for four honors classes. At the start of the second semester, there were eighty students enrolled — a difference of sixteen students. *Sixteen students from our school had dropped out of the honors algebra program by the end of the first semester.*

I was told that we have a problem over here: that our students do not come to Hillcrest as adequately prepared as students from other middle schools; that it takes our students a semester of hard work in order to catch up. Obviously, some never do. We had thirty-three students recommended for the Honors program in the Fall; sixteen students continued the second semester — a drop out rate of almost 50 per cent.

Russ, when I see eighth grade students sitting around in your algebra class not doing anything, I find it very difficult to look at the information from Hillcrest and find excuses for our showing there. I know our program could be more demanding. What pains me is that you have everything it takes to be a fine teacher. You are the most popular teacher with the students. You certainly have the math background and I've observed some excellent teaching techniques on occasion. What I do not see is a program challenging enough, that demands from our students. Students work at their own pace with your support; the slower students set the pace or the pace is set by your assignments on the board and whatever else you may ask. In my opinion, you put too much emphasis on the students' ability to teach themselves without your support and not enough emphasis on your role as a teacher teaching an algebra class. We have discussed this before. I do not feel there is any commitment from you to change our algebra program or your approach in the classroom.

I want to see:

1   More class time spent on teacher directed instruction (for example, the working of examples or homework problems on the chalkboard).
2   Less class time spent completing assignments on the blackboard — students can do this at home.
3   Homework assignments reviewed by the teacher and students together.
4   Students called upon to demonstrate their proficiency with problems — not just the teacher telling them how to do every problem.

Follow-up surveys

Each year the district selects one or two curriculum areas for intensive review. As a part of this review process, each school prepares a follow-up survey and sends it to students who have graduated. The major objective of this survey is to identify strengths and weaknesses in the school's instructional programs. The results of this annual survey are incorporated into the teacher evaluation program and shared with teachers during the evaluation process. The following memo and attachments illustrate how these survey results are sometimes used:

Inter-Office Memo

To: Russ Brown
From: J. Jones
(18 attachments)

We recently surveyed Hillcrest High School freshmen regarding how well our school had prepared them for the math program at Hillcrest. To date eighteen students have responded.

I am passing these comments to you. Since I don't seem to be able to reach you with these concerns, maybe these student comments will.

. . .

Attachment #8.

1 *In your opinion, how well were you prepared at Ocean View Middle School for the math program at Hillcrest High School?*

Although math has never been one of my 'better' subjects, I feel *I should be doing better at Hillcrest*. I do *not* feel like Ocean View did a satisfactory job in preparing me for Hillcrest. [Mr. Brown was much too lenient (sic.), especially on test days. In my class, cheating was very apparant (sic.)] I was *told to go to algebra honors* at Hillcrest, and followed through with the recommendation. When I got there, I felt literally *helpless*, not knowing three-quarters of what they were discussing. I know I am not a dumb person, but this is not good for the self-esteem. It seemed like the Ocean View students were the only ones who did not understand. I got taken out of that class and placed into a regular algebra class where I am improving slowly.

2 *What suggestions or comments would you make regarding the math program at Ocean View Middle School?*

When I was there, the grading was *far too lenient* (sic.). Eighth graders should *not* be put into algebra honors at Hillcrest unless they are *positive* they can handle it. It's really a bad feeling — knowing you are almost the only one who does not understand.

In my class, we would stay on one particular thing much too long. It was apparant (sic.) everyone understood, and we could have gone on to something else, yet we kept repeatedly doing the same thing. Many others who I have talked to felt the same way.

In closing, I would like to say that with a little more discipline and hard work, future students will be better prepared than us.

Mary Heinz
_____

Student's Signature (optional)

. . .

Attachment #15.

1 *In your opinion, how well were you prepared at Ocean View Middle School for the math program at Hillcrest High School?*

I do not feel that I was adequately prepared for algebra at Hillcrest. Mr. Brown didn't spend enough time explaining 'how to do' the processes of algebra. I've done very well in the algebra program at Hillcrest probably because of the help from my father.

2 *What suggestions or comments would you make regarding the math program at Ocean Views Middle School?*

Lots of time should be spent in explanation. What good does it do to look in the back of the book for the answers if you don't understand the problems in the first place?

Mark Breci
_____

Student's Signature (optional)

Needs assessments

In addition to follow-up surveys of former students, the schools in Ocean View conduct an annual needs assessment to solicit the opinions of current students and their parents regarding the instructional program. They are asked to rate the importance of each curricular area on a five-point scale (1 being low and 5 being high) and to rate the performance of the area on the same five-point scale. Students and parents also are encouraged to write additional comments and reactions if they have any to express. These ratings and comments are summarized for each teacher and may be included in the year-end evaluation of the teacher's performance. By way of illustration, we have reproduced the following comments from the spring evaluation of Mrs. Long, a sixth-grade science teacher:

Evaluator's Report

I am sharing the results of our annual needs assessment with Mrs. Long because I am worried about the science program. The sixth grade results are especially disturbing; the rankings are as follows:

	Importance	Performance
Parents	4.6	2.6
Students	3.2	2.7

Parents and students alike rate the sixth grade science program the lowest of any academic program in the school. Moreover, there is a big gap between the importance parents attach to the sixth grade science program and their evaluation of its performance.[3]

The written comments of parents and students are generally unfavourable as well:

'I think the school is doing real well! Except for science where I am barely learning anything.'

'Science isn't performing well. Science should be made more interesting than it has been. I think we should have a day in science where you ask the teacher stuff you don't understand.'

'In science I feel that Mrs. Long is very ununderstandable (sic.) and that her class is very complicated.'

In the sixth grade science program we don't get much out of it.'

'Science is too boring. She should do more than just lecture all the time. She also should get to know students a little more — like learn their names.'

'I've never worked so hard and cared so little about a subject in all of my life.'

. . .

These negative comments must be balanced with supportive statements from two parents who stated:

'My son enjoys the lecture/college-type approach to the science curriculum.'

'Our son appreciated Mrs. Long's coverage of astronomy; it was a provocative and stimulating experience.'

Both of these students are exceptional achievers.

Based on these results and my own observations in your class I would have to conclude that:

1   Your curriculum is geared toward the 'exceptional' student. (Recently I tried to take notes during a film you showed but couldn't because of the technical language being used. I was interested in the recommended level of the film and consulted the County Audio Visual catalog. The film was rated for *Senior High to Adult*. It definitely is *not* a film for sixth grade students.)

2   Those students who cannot learn orally, abstractly, or who cannot take copious notes find your class overwhelming.

3   That the emphasis is on the lecture approach rather than on the project, discovery approach.

4   That your curriculum has not changed much in the last fifteen years.

Parent comments

Besides soliciting opinions from parents about the instructional program, Ocean View administrators also encourage unsolicited comments. In the words of the Superintendent, 'Our parents are very concerned with academic progress, have high expectations, and voice their concerns often'. These parental comments may creep into the evaluation process. If the principal judges these comments to be reliable, (s)he may place them in the teacher's personnel file and use them in the year-end evaluation of the teacher as long as the comments or complaints are dated and signed by the parents.

Resources

Principals are provided with an array of resources to carry out their responsibilities for working with those teachers whose performance is either unsatisfactory or in need of improvement. These resources serve different functions. If the principals' objective is to improve a teacher's performance, they have discretionary funds which can be spent for this purpose and access to a full-time staff development specialist. Principals may also enlist the aid of a counselor if they need assistance in coping with the emotional demands inherent in this process. If legal action becomes necessary, principals may consult with an attorney. Finally, principals may request counseling services for the teacher if they believe that (s)he is ready to consider early retirement or other types of employment.

Staff development specialist

To assist the principals in meeting the Board's commitment to the SOS Foundation, the district employed a full-time staff development specialist for a fixed term of three years. This individual was an exceptional teacher who was highly respected by the teaching and administrative staff. He worked intensively with the marginal teachers in the district during this period. He was supportive of these teachers, showed a genuine interest in their improvement, provided them with specific, non-evaluative feedback about was happening in their classrooms, engaged them in considering other alternatives, and taught demonstration lessons. At no time was he working with more than five teachers; consequently, he was able to provide them with his undivided attention over an extended period. No one doubted either his sincerity or his skill; yet, few teachers showed sufficient improvement to warrant retention. One of the most respected teachers in the district characterized the situation as follows:

> He was really sharp, and his heart was in the right place. But after a year or so, the teachers started to refer to him as Father Damien. He really tried to help the teachers who were in trouble, but they, like the lepers in Molokai, rarely got well. As I recall, only one was turned around; the rest didn't make it. (Note: Damien De Veuster was a Roman Catholic Priest who devoted much of his life to caring for the lepers at Molokai, Hawaii, during the mid 1800s. He comforted these poor souls and ministered to their spiritual and medical needs, but there was no cure for their malady.)

Discretionary funds

Principals in the Ocean View school district are allotted ample financial resources to work with teachers who are deemed in need of improvement. The middle school Principal summed up the district's philosophy in this way,

> The Board and Superintendent offer us all the resources we need to help a teacher succeed, and they expect to have an exemplary instructional program or to see solid evidence that we are on our way to having one. If not, the teacher must go.

When a teacher is in difficulty, principals use these resources in a variety of ways to effect improvement in a teacher's performance. They purchase instructional equipment (even a new science lab) and materials which a teacher may need to modernize his/her approach. If a teacher has an outmoded curriculum or relies heavily on the lecture method, (s)he may be hired in the summer to develop units of instruction and pupil-centered activities or projects. Subject-matter specialists are employed as consultants to work intensively with teachers for a week or more. Individuals are also hired to help teachers prepare high quality dittoed materials and overhead transparencies. Substitutes are hired to enable a teacher to attend workshops that center on the types of problems (s)he may be having. Aides are employed to organize the teacher's classroom; they straighten the teacher's files, inventory the materials that clutter the room, label these materials, and store them in such a way that they can be easily accessed by the teacher. In short, when a teacher is in difficulty, principals place him or her in intensive care. 'When we are finished, no one including the teacher, ever doubts that we made a concerted effort to save the teacher', said one of the elementary principals.

Prospective counseling

Communicating career-threatening information to subordinates is a painful, unpleasant task for administrators, including the principals in Ocean View. To help them cope effectively with the emotional ordeal, the administration relies on a technique that has been used successfully in various settings to prepare people for emotional confrontations. This technique is prospective counseling.[4] It has been used in the field of medicine to assist patients who have decided to undergo major surgery and are awaiting the operation (Egbert *et al.*, 1964; Schmitt and Woolridge, 1973), to prepare women for childbirth (Levy and McGee, 1975), and to help hospitalized patients about to undergo a disagreeable medical examination (Johnson and Leventhal, 1974). Prospective counseling also has been used in business to prepare potential employees for the undesirable features of the jobs for which they are

Edwin M. Bridges

applying (Wanous, 1973). In each instance, the goal of prospective counseling is to let people experience the unpleasant consequences in advance and to make plans for dealing more effectively with the situation when it actually occurs.

In Ocean View, principals may enlist the services of a counselor who is on the district payroll. This individual is familiar with the teachers in the district and is used in role-playing situations with the principal. If the principal anticipates that (s)he may have a difficult conference with a teacher, the principal and the counselor role-play the conference. The counselor attempts to respond in the way that the teacher is likely to respond. Immediately after the role-playing, the counselor and the principal critique what has happened. If necessary, the principal revises his or her approach in light of this exchange. In the words of a principal who often uses prospective counseling, 'Role playing is a major part of evaluation. I always rehearse tough conferences with the counselor. It's a big help and really builds my confidence.'

Legal assistance

One of the barriers to confronting and dealing forthrightly with incompetent teachers is the array of legal rights possessed by tenured and probationary teachers. Principals need the assistance of a competent attorney if they are to navigate this legal minefield successfully. The administration in Ocean View recognizes this need and attempts to meet it. Whenever a principal senses that (s)he may be forced to take legal action against an unsatisfactory teacher, (s)he may enlist the advice and counsel of an attorney who specializes in personnel matters. This attorney acquaints principals with the teacher's rights and the statutory timelines that must be followed in evaluating, assisting, and disciplining the teacher for poor performance. The attorney also is available to assist principals in preparing their documentation and in analyzing the strengths and weaknesses of the case that is being built against the teacher. If a 90-day notice of deficiency or incompetence needs to be issued, the attorney drafts the legal document to ensure that it complies with the law. Since principals lack adequate formal training in the legal aspects of teacher evaluation (Groves, 1985), the legal assistance that is provided to Ocean View principals in anticipation of future legal action represents an important resource, and it is used whenever legal issues arise.

136

Counseling services

At the point where teachers begin to consider another career or early retirement, the district has an employee assistance program which provides a range of counseling services to these teachers. This program offers financial, personal, psychological, and vocational counseling to teachers in an effort to facilitate their transition from teaching to other pursuits. If a teacher elects to seek other employment, (s)he may receive outplacement counseling if (s)he requests it. This type of counseling is often used in business to assist displaced executives (Brammer and Humberger, 1984) and includes professional assistance in preparing resumés, creating job search plans, and preparing for job interviews. All of these counseling services are provided by a Los Angeles firm under a contract with the Ocean View Elementary District. This firm charges $2000 to $3000 per client depending on the services rendered. According to the Superintendent,

> This program has been very successful and very positive for both the teacher and the district. We even include the teacher's spouse if it's necessary. In one case a teacher was reluctant to quit because his wife didn't want him at home and wanted the money. But with the counseling, she was convinced that they could make it financially. This program really helps teachers get in touch with reality and assess their situation in a rational manner.

Accountability

In most school districts principals spend less time on managing instruction than they believe they should. The principals in Ocean View deviate from this common pattern because of the climate created by the Superintendent and the Board of Education. One of the principals described this climate in the following words:

> Quality instruction is the number one priority of the Board and the Superintendent. They have made their policy clear to the principals. The burden of evaluating teachers and improving instruction rests on our shoulders. When a new principal is hired, the superintendent makes sure that the person is an outstanding teacher and a rigorous evaluator. Once hired principals are expected to spend lots of time in classrooms. If

teachers are having problems, we're expected to help them. If they don't improve, it's our responsibility to ease them out. The Board gives us all the resources we need to get the job done and holds us accountable for doing it.

The Board uses both formal and informal means to evaluate principals. Twice a year the Board meets in closed sessions with the superintendent and the three principals to discuss the performance of the teaching staff. These meetings generally last five to six hours. Principals review the strengths and weaknesses of each teacher. If a teacher is having serious problems, the principal provides an in-depth evaluation of the teacher's difficulties and describes the steps which the principal has taken, or is taking, to overcome them. An attorney is also present at these meetings to answer any legal questions which may arise. The Board uses these occasions as one way of assessing how well principals are implementing its concern for quality instruction.

Principals are also evaluated in a more formal and systematic manner by the Board and the Superintendent. These annual evaluations follow a management-by-objectives format and are based on the principal's job description. The results of these evaluations influence the principal's salary and employment status within the district. Several years ago the Board and Superintendent released a principal who continued to inflate the evaluations of weak teachers after being advised to provide more accurate assessments. Currently principals can receive several thousand dollars for superior performance in upgrading their school's instructional program. This amount is added to the across-the-board salary increases granted to all certificated employees.

Induced Exits

The major reason for initiating this aggressive and comprehensive approach to teacher evaluation was to reduce the size of the Ocean View teaching staff on the basis of performance rather than seniority. Impetus for this thrust came from the parents who formed the SOS Foundation to fund the additional costs associated with this bold action. Four years after this program was initiated there were nine fewer teachers in the district. None of these teachers was laid off on the basis of seniority. All nine were induced to resign or to request early retirement; and in the judgment of the principals and the Superintendent, these teachers were the weakest ones in the district.

The administration exerted considerable pressure on these teachers during this period while simultaneously providing intensive and extensive remedial assistance. Principals were forthright in communicating the district's performance expectations and in letting teachers know whether they were making satisfactory progress in meeting these expectations. Perhaps because of the district's concerted effort to salvage these teachers, some did not realize that they were in serious trouble until a 90-day notice of deficiency or incompetence was served. Most teachers (seven of the nine who left) did not agree to resign or to retire early until the administration applied this type of pressure. The administration never found it necessary to issue a notice of intent to dismiss, the most intense pressure that can be exerted.

'After these notices (90-day) are served, most teachers are willing to discuss alternatives to classroom teaching', said the Superintendent. In his opinion,

> It is important not to discuss these alternatives until the teacher is ready to accept the advice of an administrator. If an administrator pushes his views too early, the teacher may be turned off and resent the alternatives proposed.

Although the Superintendent serves the notice of incompetency to the teachers, he plays a conciliatory role and counsels with them. 'It's the Principal who plays the tough guy role throughout the entire process', observed the Superintendent. During the negotiations which follow the issuance of the 90-day notice, the Superintendent attempts to discover what the teacher's needs are and to figure out the ways in which these needs can be met, wholly or in part. This process of give-and-take ordinarily takes two or three months to complete.

The union has been a silent ally of the Ocean View administration over the past four years. In the words of a former teacher representative,

> The remediation efforts are sincere. The district tries to improve performance. There is some paranoia and hard feelings about what has happened, and teachers might complain at some point. But, we had some bad teachers, and the problems needed to be addressed.

According to the Superintendent,

> CTA (California Teachers' Association) has been very helpful in this district. They provide constructive comments to help the

teacher improve. They even told some teachers, 'You are going to have to make some changes in your teaching or quit. The district will dismiss you if you don't'.

The union has never filed a grievance to protest an evaluation or a disciplinary action during this period. It remains convinced that the administration has treated teachers fairly.

Thus far, the district administration has used three types of inducements to obtain the resignations and early retirements. These are employment as a consultant, outplacement counseling, and medical coverage at district expense. The district is not wedded to these alternatives, however. In the words of the Superintendent,

> We are now considering a lump sum payment to get rid of one teacher. We will investigate every alternative to get rid of weak teachers. If we don't need all of our teachers because of declining enrollments, the mediocre ones will leave, not the lowest in seniority.

The Aftermath

Public confidence in the Ocean View Elementary School District has soared. Prior to the district's efforts to improve the quality of its teaching staff, parents withdrew their children from the public schools and enrolled them in private schools which they perceived to be of higher academic quality. When parents learned that the weakest teachers were leaving the Ocean View district, many of these parents re-enrolled their children in the public schools. Moreover, approximately fifty families from neighboring school districts arranged inter-district transfers so that their children could attend the Ocean View public schools. One mother drove her daughter one-and-a-half hours each way so that she could go to school in this community; another family bought an expensive piece of property in Ocean View for the same reason. In the words of the Board President,

> Our district has met the challenge of the private schools. Public education has met the competition and surpassed it.

The SOS Foundation continues to provide financial support for the Ocean View schools. However, this money is no longer used to underwrite the staff development program. The money goes into the district's general fund and is used to fund programs that have been eliminated in many districts as the financial noose tightened. Approximately $100,000 a year are raised to support a program for gifted students, to fund acquisitions for the school libraries, to provide counseling services, and to underwrite the costs of a music program.

Summary

The Ocean View Elementary School District further illustrates how organizational structure and environmental factors influence administrative responses to incompetent teachers. Prior to the need for retrenchment, administrators in this relatively small district were inclined to be lenient when evaluating teachers. During this period of prosperity, administrators also used various escape hatches to sidestep the problems posed by incompetent teachers. To avoid parental complaints, administrators assigned the poor performers to teach electives and physical education. However, enrollment declines and a financial crunch altered these practices. When district officials announced their intention to lay off two highly regarded teachers who happened to have the least seniority, parents strongly objected. They wanted the district administration to prune the staff by dismissing the worst teachers and formed a foundation to pay for the legal costs associated with this drastic action. The Superintendent and Board of Education countered with a similarly bold proposal. They agreed to institute a rigorous program of teacher evaluation, to undertake intensive efforts to improve the weakest teachers, and to induce them to leave the district if they failed to improve. The Board and Superintendent also agreed to retain all teachers until this program had been fully implemented; future staff reductions would be based on performance, not seniority.[5] The parents accepted this counterproposal and agreed to underwrite the costs of this plan through the SOS (Save Our Schools) Foundation.

During the first four years of implementing this program, the Ocean View school officials worked with the ten weakest teachers in the district. These teachers, unlike their counterparts in other districts, received intensive and comprehensive assistance to overcome their difficulties. The results of these salvage attempts were not much different, however. Only one of the ten teachers improved sufficiently to warrant retention. The rest of the teachers were induced to submit resignations or to request early retirements. Seven of these nine teachers did not agree to leave until the administration applied considerable pressure by issuing 90-day notices of incompetency. To ease their transition into retirement or other lines of work, these teachers often received outplacement counseling, medical coverage, or employment as a consultant. Union officials cooperated with the administration in helping these teachers to improve and in persuading them to leave when they failed to do so. The Superintendent handled the negotiations leading to these induced exits and acted as a counselor in the process even though he personally delivered the 90-day notices. As a result of these actions, the Ocean View schools regained the confidence of the general public, and they are now regarded as being equal to or better than the private schools in the area.[6]

Notes

1 The California Teachers' Association is affiliated with the National Education Association and not the American Federation of Teachers.
2 For example, the teacher 'will develop and use a collection of graded, creative, challenging, math problems' and 'will utilize the "spiral" approach to teach and review math concepts'. Accomplishment of these objectives will be assessed by classroom observation and a review of the materials prepared by the teacher.
3 The evaluator is comparing scores on two different scales; one scale reflects a utility and the other effectiveness. These two scales are conceptually independent so it is not clear why they are being compared. If the importance of sex education is 2 and effectiveness is 3, there still may be a teaching problem. On the other hand, if science is rated 4.8 in importance and 3.8 in effectiveness, there may or may not be a teaching problem. The reader should be wary of using these scales in the way in which they are being used in this particular instance.
4 Prospective counseling is my term. Janis and Mann (1977) refer to the technique as emotional inoculation.
5 Johnson (1980) has done a study of performance-based layoff policies in several school districts. Contrary to our research, she uncovered a number of problems associated with the implementation of these formal layoff policies. The reader may wish to read Johnson's report to learn about the policies and the problems which she found.
6 Near the completion of the interview study, Barry Groves, my research assistant, inadvertently learned about the high rate of induced exits in the Ocean View Elementary School District. I asked him to collect data about what was happening in this district to see if the conditions and responses corresponded to the pattern that was emerging in our interviews with school administrators throughout the state of California.

Chapter 7

Education at the Crossroads

Throughout this book I have striven to provide a lucid, dispassionate description and analysis of how administrators respond to the problem of teacher incompetence and of the conditions which shape these responses. In this chapter I feel obligated to move beyond what is and offer a glimpse into what might occur in the near future. A window of opportunity is opening for the public schools, but this opportunity is fraught with perils as well as possibilities. By discussing the opportunity, the perils and the possibilities which loom over the educational horizon, I hope to engage school officials and teachers in a reasoned consideration of local personnel policies and practices. If this book stimulates reflection on what is, what might be, and what should be, it will have served its purposes.

The Window of Opportunity

For a decade or more the public schools experienced a decline in consumer demand. Between 1972 and 1982, forty-three states plus the District of Columbia suffered enrollment declines. The average loss in student enrollment was 14 per cent nationwide (Feistritzer, 1983). Most of the decline was due to a substantial drop in the number of school-age (5-17) children during this period. The size of the teaching force also decreased in many areas. In sixteen states plus the District of Columbia the average number of teachers declined by 9.5 per cent; five additional states remained in a near steady state (i.e., the size of the teaching force grew by less than 3 per cent).

The trend began reversing itself in 1984. Since that date, enroll-ment has risen each year and is projected to increase annually until 1998 (*Digest of Education Statistics*, 1990). These enrollment increases, combined with teacher retirements and resignations, will require 371,000 teachers to be hired during the decade of the 1990s. This major influx of teachers provides the public schools with an oppor-tunity to institute policies which will ensure that future generations of students will be taught by fully competent teachers.

The Perils

Simply put, the major peril is that history may repeat itself in those districts which attach little importance to teacher evaluation and to the granting of tenure. The following imaginary, but realistic, scenario illustrates how this repetition may unfold. It is patterned in large part after the analysis presented in chapters 2, 3 and 4.

Pre-Tenure

The Uniontown School District announces that it will be hiring ten elementary teachers. School officials prepare a brochure about the school district and mail it, along with the following announcement, to local university placement offices:

JOB ANNOUNCEMENT

College graduates with a bachelor's degree in elementary education. Excellent communication skills required. Need solid background in English, math, science and social studies. Back-ground in music or art also desired. Starting salary $16,100 with a guarantee of annual increases for fourteen years. Cost of living raises are likely but not guaranteed. Fringe benefits include district contributions to pension, medical plan, and dental plan.

Several weeks pass, and the Personnel Director starts to fret. There are only fifteen applicants for ten openings. She decides to extend the deadline for applications. Several more weeks pass. Only two addition-al applications are submitted so she decides to invite the seventeen applicants in for interviews. Two of them decline the invitation; they have accepted offers elsewhere. The Personnel Director looks at the size and the quality of the applicant pool. She recalls from her course in personnel that an unfavorable selection ratio means trouble later. She quickly dismisses the thought from her mind and recommends ten of the fifteen applicants for employment.

School opens and the Principal at Uniontown Elementary School greets his four new teachers. He gives them a brief, impromptu introduction to the school and then hands them a grade book, a set of keys and a faculty handbook. During the first few weeks, he tours the school and makes an effort to eavesdrop outside their classrooms. Occasionally he enters their classrooms for a brief observation (five to ten minutes) and follows the visit with a report punctuated with glowing generalities. The rest of the time the Principal works in his office. He reads his mail, answers his correspondence, attends to his phone calls, and holds numerous scheduled and unscheduled meetings. His day is hectic and fragmented, and he considers himself fortunate if he can spend more than ten uninterrupted minutes on any problem or activity.

The fall term ends, and the Principal receives a phone call from the Superintendent's office. Teacher evaluation reports are due in two weeks. He decides to block out some time to complete these reports and to confer with his teachers. The four new teachers seem to be doing all right. On the surface they appear to be having only the kinds of problems any beginner has. The Principal decides to be a real source of encouragement and praises each one for the fine job (s)he is doing. All four receive ratings of outstanding or satisfactory in every area of performance.

This pattern repeats itself over the next year and a half, and the Principal recommends the four teachers for tenure. Deep down he senses that one or two of these teachers are not really that good, but he tells himself, 'The next ones could be even worse'. (A common rationalization used in the 1960s, a period of teacher shortage.)[1]

Post-Tenure

Business as usual

Several years pass; not much has changed. Three of the four recently tenured teachers remain at the Uniontown Elementary School. One teacher, the most talented of the four, has resigned to pursue a more lucrative and prestigious career in the field of business. The Principal continues to work at a harried pace, but now he realizes that his previous doubts are being confirmed. Two of the four teachers whom he recommended for tenure are not doing well. Fortunately, only a few parents have complained so the Principal feels that the situation is bearable. In any event he is not totally ignoring what is happening. He visits these classrooms whenever he can find the time and follows up with a report based on his observations. There are problems, but he chooses to use a positive approach. He casts his criticisms in a positive light, emphasizes the need for continued professional growth, and provides the teachers with words of encouragement. Despite his efforts, the two teachers do not show much, if any, improvement. 'I don't seem to be able to reach them', the Principal says to himself. However, he continues to give these teachers the benefit-of-the-doubt on their annual evaluations in hopes that they, like fine wine, will improve with age.

Altered states

The Principal eventually retires, and his successor, a woman in her mid-thirties, is a first-year Principal who is determined to make Uniontown the best elementary school in the district.[2] She sets priorities and ensures that her crowded weekly schedule allows time for classroom observations and follow-up conferences. She is dismayed to learn that two members of her staff are doing so poorly in the classroom and phones the Personnel Director to arrange a meeting to discuss these problem teachers. At this meeting the Personnel Director reviews the files of these teachers and says with a shrug of her shoulders, 'There's not much we can do. Both of these teachers have reasonably strong evaluations over the past twelve years. We would look foolish if we tried to dismiss them'. The Principal is outraged and states firmly, 'I don't want these teachers in my school. They aren't any good, and I don't intend to put up with them'. The Personnel Director responds, 'I know how you feel. Let me discuss the matter with the Superintendent, and I'll get back to you in a week or so'.

Later that week the Personnel Director meets with the Superintendent to explain the situation. Both agree that something must be done, and they begin to review the possibilities: transfer to another school, reassignment as a substitute teacher or as a home-study teacher, and reassignment to the central office to work on a special project or a federally-supported program. At this point all appear to represent viable alternatives.

Immediately following the meeting with the Superintendent, the Personnel Director confers with the Principal. During the conference the Personnel Director outlines the plan of operation for the next few months. The Principal is to continue her observations of these two teachers. These observations are to be followed by written reports which document the deficiencies and the remediation which has been prescribed. The Principal is expected to confer with these teachers and to clarify what they should do to improve their performance. After each conference, the Principal should prepare a written report and send a copy to the teacher. If the teachers fail to improve, the Personnel Director will meet with them to discuss other possibilities. 'At that point', says the Director of Personnel, 'they will be eager to consider other options'. Five months later, one teacher agrees to become a home-study teacher; the other accepts an assignment in the central office.

Diminished capacity

A few more years pass; enrollments start to fall and the district experiences a financial crunch. The district institutes an early retirement plan. Teachers who resign or retire are not replaced. The resignations and the retirements, however, do not keep pace with the enrollment declines. Teachers with the least seniority are laid off, and teachers, like the two tenured teachers on special assignment, are returned to regular teaching positions.

When these two teachers re-enter the classroom, serious problems arise. Their principals start to receive parental complaints. In a few months the trickle turns into a flood. The principals meet with the Personnel Director, and the three of them agree on a course of action. Initially the principals will attempt to salvage these two teachers. Because the rescue operations may be unsuccessful, the principals should lay the groundwork for dismissal. They are to do the following: (a) observe the teacher; (b) be forthright in their criticisms; (c) prescribe what should be done by the teacher to improve; (d) provide the teacher with assistance (for example release the teacher to visit other class-rooms and offer the teacher an opportunity to participate in profess-ional development activities); (e) withhold lavish praise for modest improvement; and (f) document, document, document. If the salvage attempt fails, the Personnel Director will meet with the teachers and try to secure an early retirement.

For the rest of the school year and half of the next, the two principals work intensively with these two veteran teachers; however,

147

neither improves. Both are very defensive and resist what is happening to them. The principals and the Personnel Director decide to issue a 90-day notice of incompetency if the Superintendent and the Board of Education approve the action. The notice is served, and the principals step up the pressure. They increase the frequency of observations and the flow of negative communications. Still there are no signs of improvement.

Near the expiration of the 90-day notice the Personnel Director arranges to meet separately with each of the teachers. Prior to these meetings she confers with the union representative and lays out the case against the teachers. The union representative agrees to assist in persuading the teachers to retire. At the meeting with the teacher and the union representative, the Personnel Director looks directly at the teacher and says, 'I'm sorry, but it just hasn't worked out. You haven't improved. We intend to issue a dismissal notice and charge you with incompetence. However, before taking this action, we want to let you know our intentions and to give you an opportunity to consider other possibilities. You have taught a long time in this district, and you may not want to end your career in a dismissal hearing before the Commission on Professional Competence. I'd like to encourage you to discuss this matter with your union representative. Let me know what you want to do. I'm willing to consider any possibilities which you might suggest'.

Two days later the two teachers schedule another meeting with the Personnel Director. Each expresses an interest in early retirement. One is in ill health and wants the district to continue paying for her Blue Cross-Blue Shield health plan. The other teacher indicates that he would like to be hired as a consultant until he reaches age 65 because he is having financial problems. The Personnel Director, with the approval of the Superintendent and the Board of Education, agrees to the requests. She also offers to place their forthcoming evaluations in her own personal file rather than in each teacher's personnel record. The teachers appear to appreciate this gesture. History has indeed repeated itself in a district that attaches little importance to teacher evaluation.

The Possibilities

However, history does not necessarily repeat itself. A teacher shortage may not reoccur; even if it does, the shortage may be spread unevenly across school districts, teaching specialties (for example, special education, science, and math), and grade levels (elementary versus high school). Moreover, the personnel policies and practices which school districts adopt in response to the current concern about teacher quality may avert many of the responses detailed in chapters 2 through 5. These same policies also may minimize the detrimental impact of retrenchment when, and if, it once again strikes the schools.

In the scenario that follows, a set of policies is outlined which attempts to grapple with the realities commonly faced by local districts in dealing with the problem of teacher incompetence. The policies and practices which are sketched in this scenario stem from two sources: (i) the research that was conducted in school districts throughout the state of California; and (ii) a review of the literature that bears on the problems of tenure and poor performance.

Pre-Tenure

The Unity School District has entered a new era. Enrollments are rising, and the teaching staff is finally expanding. This year the district will be hiring six elementary teachers. The Personnel Director prepares a brochure about the district and the community it serves. He mails copies, along with an announcement of the job openings, to the placement agencies of colleges and universities throughout the state. As an afterthought, he places a 3″ × 3″ ad in the local newspapers.

Weeks pass, and much to the surprise of the Personnel Director he has received thirty applications for the six positions. He rushes into the Superintendent's office. 'Laura, for the first time in several years we have the opportunity to upgrade our teaching staff if we institute some major changes in our teacher evaluation program. Are you interested?' She replies, 'Yes. Put together your views on the subject, and get them to me as soon as possible. By the way, I want to know what the trade-offs are. Nothing comes without a price'.

The Personnel Director returns to his office and starts to compose the following memo (see note number 3 for references and additional comments relating to the contents of this memo):[3]

To: Laura Jones, Superintendent
From: Sam Bradbury, Director of Certificated Personnel
Subject: Teacher evaluation

As a follow-up to our recent conversation, I am sharing with you my views about the following five issues:

1. the selection of teachers;
2. the importance of the tenure decision;
3. the evaluation of probationary teachers;
4. the trade-offs; and
5. the next steps.

Teacher Selection

We have thirty applicants for six positions. The information which we have on these people is not very helpful. Each of these placement files reads like an obituary: born in Hamlet, USA; went to school at; married to so and so; active in such and such organizations; ad nauseum. The recommendations of the student teaching supervisors and the college professors resemble the teacher evaluations of some of our principals. The statements are filled with nothing but generalities (mostly glowing) and double-talk. We need better information on which to base our decisions; I recommend that we do the following:

(a)   Ask three of our best teachers and three of our best teacher evaluators to review the recommendations in these placement files and to prepare a memo that we will send to university placement officers. This memo should identify statements which our teachers and evaluators consider meaningless and should provide examples of the kinds of information which this team finds helpful. We need to make clear to these placement officers that their candidates will be at a distinct disadvantage if their recommendations are non-informative.

(b)   Encourage, if not require, newly trained applicants to submit video-tapes (30–45 minutes) of themselves presenting a lesson during their student teaching.

(c)   Require the finalists for teaching positions to prepare a lesson based on an objective formulated by the selection team(s). Each finalist will be expected to teach the lesson to a small group of students while being observed by members of the selection committee.

Importance of the Tenure Decision

Based on years of experience in this district, I think that we have been too casual about the tenure decision, and we have paid a high price for our easygoing attitude. It's clear to me now that the tenure decision is the last opportunity we have to enforce high performance standards on our teaching staff. Once they receive tenure, they have to be a blatant failure before we can get rid of them. Every time we make a mistake, it means lots of problems down the road. Students get shortchanged; parents eventually complain; and administrators wind up spending an inordinate amount of time and energy trying to rescue the unsalvageable. I think that we can avoid most of these problems by treating the tenure decision for what it is, the single most important personnel decision we make. Before we assume a million dollar obligation to a teacher and limit our future institutional flexibility, we need considerable assurance that our decision to grant tenure is the right one.

Evaluation of Probationary Teachers

I think that we should redesign our teacher evaluation system to reflect the importance of the tenure decision. Our resources (chiefly time, energy, people and money) are limited, and we should allocate them where we are likely to receive the greatest return. In my judgment, the evaluation of probationary teachers and the decision to grant or deny tenure should receive the top priority. In redesigning our system to reflect the overriding importance of evaluating probationary teachers, we should be hard on the standards but soft on the people. The features of our evaluation system should echo these concerns.

Hard on the Standards

The most problematic issue is standards. I'm inclined to make it as hard for teachers to obtain tenure as it is for them to lose tenure. Once teachers have acquired tenure, we can't dismiss them unless we can prove that they are incompetent. Dismissal isn't easy because we must prove by a preponderance of the evidence that the teacher is really incompetent. This standard of proof is the same one that we should use in making the tenure decision. I dusted off one of the legal references which I haven't used for several years to find out what this term means. According to one expert on school law,

> The courts have often defined the term 'preponderance of the evidence', since it is the general standard used in civil cases. The phrase probably is most easily understood as meaning a majority of the evidence, or 51 per cent. It has also been defined as the greater weight of the evidence that is credible and convincing and 'best accords with reason and probability'. To prove by a preponderance of the evidence means ... that 'the evidence must when considered fairly and impartially, induce a reasonable belief that the fact in issue is true'.

His comments reveal some of the ambiguity inherent in using this standard of proof. But you know, as well as I do, that the measurement of teacher effectiveness is an inexact science. Under these conditions, it makes sense to use a standard which reflects the subjective, judgmental nature of teacher evaluation and which calls for credible, convincing evidence to support the judgment. This evidence should induce a reasonable belief that the teacher satisfactorily meets the criteria which we currently use in evaluating teachers (for example, ability to maintain discipline and impart subject matter). Moreover, the evidence should focus on the teacher's current performance and not on his or her potential to become a competent teacher. I've been burned too many times by evaluators who thought they could foretell the future.

To me fully competent means more than satisfactory performance in terms of our criteria. Fully competent signifies that the teacher possesses at least one quality which sets him/her apart from most of the teachers on our teaching staff. This quality (I choose to call it the flair factor) should be of special significance or value to some or all of our students. If the teacher lacks this flair factor (for example, special talents in art or music, ability to work with students from different racial and ethnic backgrounds, and working knowledge of another language or culture), we shouldn't consider him/her worthy of tenure.

Soft on the People

Since being hard on the standards and soft on the people sounds a bit contradictory, let me explain what I mean. Beginning teachers usually are left on their own to master the complexities of teaching. If we are going to hold these teachers accountable for meeting stringent standards, we should abandon our 'sink or swim' philosophy. During their probationary period, teachers should receive intensive care and assistance. We should help them to overcome their deficiencies and to extend their repertoire of teaching strategies (more about this later). In my experience, remediation doesn't work well with the veteran teachers, but that doesn't mean it won't work with neophytes. I'd like to see us concentrate our in-service efforts on these inexperienced teachers.

Being soft on the people also means that we should provide some assistance to the teachers who aren't granted tenure. Over the years I've been in a good position to observe what has happened to people when they lost their jobs. There is a common pattern. First, these people experience shock and disbelief; they feel like their whole world is coming to an end. Next, they become angry and are outraged at what has happened to them. Before long, they really start to doubt themselves; when this happens, they usually become depressed. Finally, they begin to consider new job possibilities and to look for work. This whole period is a seemingly endless ordeal. I feel that we should help these people cope with this difficult situation and assist them in making the transition. We've done this a time or two with our veteran teachers, and our efforts were successful. I'd like to extend this practice to the young teachers who can't meet our standards for tenure. This assistance may also help our principals enforce higher standards. Many of them are inclined to give a teacher the benefit-of-the-doubt because they feel guilty about putting the teacher out of work.

Features of the System

Designing a system of teacher evaluation which reflects the concerns I have just expressed is no simple task. It may even be more difficult to implement one. In my judgment, the system for evaluating probationary teachers should have the following features:

(1) *Commitment from the top*

No plan for evaluating teachers is going to work without the total commitment and support of the Superintendent and the Board. This commitment needs to be backed up by resources and actions. I can imagine that some of our decisions to deny tenure may generate a considerable amount of conflict. When, and if, the controversy develops, you and the Board may be subjected to lots of verbal abuse from the teacher's supporters. If the Board succumbs to this pressure and grants tenure, our principals undoubtedly will revert to their former lenient evaluation practices. We need to anticipate that a stringent tenure policy is likely to evoke some strong negative reactions and to assure our principals that top management will not cave in under the pressure.

(2) *Defensible criteria*

Currently we evaluate teachers on the basis of the following criteria: (a) knowledge of subject matter; (b) ability to impart this knowledge effectively; (c) ability to maintain classroom discipline; (d) ability to maintain a suitable classroom climate; and (e) ability to establish rapport with parents and students. These criteria are too vague to withstand judicial scrutiny. We need to identify a set of indicators for each of these criteria in an effort to let teachers and evaluators know what our expectations are. Otherwise, teachers will be struggling blindly to meet undefined and unknown performance expectations. There is an abundance of research on teaching effectiveness, and I suspect that it might be helpful to us in selecting and constructing these indicators. Our own master teachers will have a lot to offer as well.

(3) *Multiple sources of evidence*

Earlier I maintained that we should adopt 'a preponderance of the evidence' as the standard of proof for determining whether probationary teachers are competent classroom teachers. In my opinion, this evidence should be based on more than the observations of principals. Because no single source of evidence is an adequate and valid indicator of teacher effectiveness, we should use a variety of sources to evaluate probationary teachers. I think the following types of evidence are worth considering: (a) principal observations; (b) student performance; (c) teacher-made materials; (d) teacher comments on student work; (e) peer observations; (f) student ratings; and (g) parent views. Perhaps, we could even consider some radical alternatives. For example, we might give probationary teachers an opportunity to present the most persuasive case they can on behalf of their own competency in the classroom. This opportunity might stimulate them to think seriously about what it means to be a competent teacher and to look at the evidence which bears on this issue. This self-evaluation could be considered along with the other types of evidence in judging whether the preponderance of the evidence induces a reasonable belief that the teacher is in fact competent.

(4) *Staff development*

We should institute two kinds of professional assistance programs for probationary teachers, and participation in these programs should be entirely voluntary. The first of these programs would be oriented to *groups* of teachers. This Professional Development Program (PDP) would focus on strategies and techniques for dealing effectively with the common problems of beginning teachers: discipline; classroom management; lesson design; and lesson implementation. In addition, the PDP staff could demonstrate a variety of instructional strategies and introduce teachers to various ways of obtaining feedback from students about what's happening in the classroom.

The second program would be geared to *individual* teachers. My first impulse was to call this program the Staff Assistance Program, but the acronym (SAP) evoked the wrong reaction. At this point I'm inclined to call it the Instructional Assistance Program (IAP). IAP staff members would be available to work with teachers in their classrooms in whatever capacity the teacher and the staff member agreed was appropriate. Since we're not sure whether either of these programs will be effective, I'd like to enter into a collaborative relationship with one of our local universities. Perhaps, one of these would be interested in studying what is happening and providing us with clues about what works and doesn't work.

Participation in PDP and IAP should be entirely voluntary. In the past our efforts to assist teachers have involved forced-feeding. I have serious doubts about the effectiveness of requiring or urging teachers to seek help. Unless teachers want assistance and believe it's necessary, they aren't likely to profit from it. We have a responsibility to offer the assistance and to let teachers know what is available. Whether they elect to use it should be left up to them and shouldn't figure in their evaluations. Principals are inclined to be lenient with teachers who are making an all-out effort to do a good job. We want our principals to judge teachers primarily on performance and results, not effort. Good performance, not a 'good attitude', should be our overriding concern.

(5) *Personal assistance*

Over the years I have been surprised at the number of teachers who were doing poorly in the classroom because they were having personal problems. Eventually marital problems, financial hardships, family troubles, legal difficulties, and the like spill over into the classroom. If we can assist teachers in navigating these troubled waters, I am reasonably confident that we can avoid or minimize the deleterious effects of these personal problems on their classroom performance. An Employee Assistance Program (EAP) is in everybody's best interests. Private business and universities have recognized the value of these programs and have used them with good results. We should follow their lead.

The EAP should also help those teachers who don't receive tenure to cope with the disappointment and to make the transition to other employment. At this point I am uncertain about how these services should be provided. Until we know how effective they are, we might contract with outside firms for these services rather than offer them through our own personnel department.

(6) *Evaluator competence*

Principal competence in the area of teacher evaluation is a major problem. One of the reasons principals do an inadequate job in this area is that they are poorly trained by colleges and universities to handle this responsibility. To compensate for the ineffectual preparation of most administrators, we need to institute an in-service training program for those who lack the necessary skills. This program should focus on developing the following skills: (a) the ability to describe and analyze what is happening in the classroom; (b) the ability to use multiple sources of evidence in evaluating a teacher's performance; (c) the ability to communicate negative information in a direct manner; (d) the ability to conduct conferences with teachers regarding their instructional performance; (e) the ability to prepare a thorough, comprehensive review of a teacher's performance for the Tenure Committee (more about this Committee later); and (f) knowledge of the legal basis of teacher evaluation. I have purposely omitted skills in diagnosing the cause(s) of a teacher's poor performance and in prescribing remediation. If teachers are having difficulty in the classroom, it is their responsibility to seek help through our assistance programs (PDP, IAP, and EAP) and to use these services to figure out what's wrong and what can be done to correct the situation. The principal orchestrates the evaluation. However, teachers bear the responsibility for correcting the problems which have been identified in the evaluation. We need to make clear that it is their problem and that we will provide assistance but only if they want it and request it.

(7) *Sufficient resources*

This plan isn't likely to work unless our principals have the resources they need to get the job done. The most critical resource is time. The scarcity of this resource is apt to cripple any efforts on our part to institute reforms in the teacher evaluation program. One of the ways in which we can safeguard their time is to limit the number of probationary teachers assigned to any school site. If we can limit this number to two or three probationary teachers a year, principals probably can handle the increased demands. We need to be sensitive to the time problem and take whatever steps are necessary to ensure that the time is available for them to conduct thorough evaluations of the non-tenured teachers.

I also think that we should provide our evaluators with access to prospective counseling. It's an emotionally draining experience to confront teachers with negative information, and teachers often behave in unpredictable ways when they are criticized by supervisors. One of our principals rehearses potentially difficult conferences with a counselor who plays the role of the teacher. This particular principal has found these dress rehearsals really useful and recommends that we make such a service available to all evaluators.

(8) *Principal accountability*

A large number of the personnel problems which have surfaced in recent years are due in part to the evaluation practices of our principals. Some of them are inclined to be too lenient because they want to avoid unpleasantness and to promote good relationships with their teachers. We should take several steps to discourage this practice. First, we need to let principals know that the evaluation of probationary teachers is of highest priority. If something has to be slighted, it shouldn't be the evaluation of these teachers. Second, we need to review the observations and the written reports of principals and provide them with feedback about the strengths and weaknesses of these documents. Third, we should keep track of the tenure recommendations of principals and monitor how these teachers perform over time. The hits and misses of principals should be incorporated into their annual evaluations. Finally, if a tenured teacher subsequently experiences difficulty in the classroom and is referred to my office for 'counseling', I think it would be a good idea to name the person who recommended this teacher for tenure in my semi-annual report to the Board.

(9) *Tenure Committee*

To underscore the importance of tenure and to ensure a wise decision on this matter, we should institute a Tenure Committee. This newly-created Committee should consist of three persons: (a) an administrator; (b) a tenured teacher who has knowledge of the probationary teacher's grade level, subject matter and teaching context; and (c) a teacher from within the system who is appointed by the teacher's union. As I envision it, the task of these Tenure Committees is two-fold: (i) to discuss the principal's review of the teacher's performance to see if it warrants by a preponderance of the evidence the granting of tenure; and (ii) to render judgments on this issue. Each member of the Tenure Committee would be expected to declare his or her opinion (yes or no) and to state the reasons for his/her judgment. The Committee's report, along with the principal's review, would be forwarded to the Superintendent and the Board of Education for a final decision on tenure.

(10) *Faculty staffing plan*

We have gone through some hard times over the past eight years: budget squeeze, declining enrollments, layoffs, forced resignations, and involuntary early retirements. Much of the pain we experienced could have been avoided. If our predecessors had done some forward planning and considered district needs and circumstances at the time of granting tenure, they could have spared us this nightmare. I don't want to put the next generation through these same difficulties.

In recasting our approach to probationary teachers, I firmly believe we should make it explicit that the decision to grant tenure is based on (a) individual merit, *and* (b) institutional needs. Before awarding tenure, the Board should consider information about the qualifications of the teacher and information about the institution. This institutional information should be updated annually and include data like the following: number of teachers by grade level and subject matter, tenure status of these teachers, projected retirement dates for teachers, projected attrition of tenured teachers for reasons other than retirement, projected enrollments for each grade over the next five to ten years, current and projected financial resources, progress in meeting our affirmative action commitments, projected changes in the character of our student population, and implications of these changes for our curriculum and teaching staff.

If the Board takes information like this into account when making tenure decisions, I am confident that we can retain the flexibility needed to deal with future conditions and circumstances — at least the ones we can foresee. Moreover, if we begin to suspect that our flexibility is in jeopardy, we can toughen the standards for granting tenure. In that event no teacher would receive tenure unless (s)he was truly exceptional.

The Trade-Offs

There are trade-offs associated with implementation of this plan. Moreover, the costs are substantial.

Less Attention to the Evaluation and Development of our Tenured Teachers

If this proposal is implemented, we will pay markedly less attention to the performance of our tenured teachers. In my judgment we currently aren't devoting as much attention or as many resources to these teachers as we should. Nonetheless, I believe my proposal is feasible only if we spend even less. If we do neglect these teachers, there is likely to be a cost.

Recently I was reading several research reports on teacher evaluation, and the results were consistent. Evaluation does make a difference in teaching performance and student achievement. Frequency of evaluation and the imposition of sanctions (for example, 90-day notices for incompetency and forced resignations) are positively related to teaching effectiveness and student performance on statewide achievement tests. If you are interested in seeing these reports, I'll dig them out of my files.

More Time Spent on Recruitment and Selection

On the assumption that probationary teachers are more likely to be denied tenure than to be granted it, I am certain that we will be spending much more time, energy, and money on recruitment and selection. It's quite possible that 'more' may become excessive or unrealistic. Without experience I really can't be any more specific than that. Time is a scarce resource, and it could become a serious problem.

More Errors in Denying Tenure

By making it more difficult for teachers to obtain tenure, we may increase the number of erroneous tenure denials. Under my proposal teachers would not be given the benefit-of-the-doubt. It is quite conceivable that some of the teachers who are denied tenure may be late bloomers and would become fully competent teachers if they were given several more years to prove themselves.

More Strain on Probationary Teachers

The first few years of teaching are stressful for most teachers. When tenure becomes more difficult to obtain, these probationary teachers will experience an added strain. Moreover, it's quite possible that these teachers will resent the prospects of being released when they realize that they are equal to or better than some of the teachers who already have tenure. If this resentment occurs, we could have a serious morale problem on our hands.

More Money

Right now we are living on a shoe string. Even if we reallocated some of our existing resources to this plan, there probably wouldn't be enough money to underwrite it. We might solve this problem by emulating some of our neighboring districts which have been successful in establishing educational foundations. Local citizens seem willing to make tax deductible contributions for worthy purposes like upgrading teacher quality. If we can't increase income, we might be able to reduce costs by cooperating with other districts. Some features of this plan (for example, in-service training for administrators and a Professional Development Program for teachers) can be funded and jointly shared by several districts.

Next Steps

If you aren't overwhelmed by the trade-offs which I have foreshadowed, I'd like to share this memo with the Board, the leaders of the teachers' union, and the principals. My previous experience with the union suggests that it would be a mistake to soften the proposal in anticipation of a negative reaction. The vast majority of teachers in this district are competent, dedicated individuals who don't want marginal or incompetent teachers in their profession. Moreover, our teachers will have their own views about how to improve the processes for awarding tenure in this district. I'd like to hear these views before we reach closure on this important issue. After you have digested the contents of this proposal, let's talk about what you think are the appropriate next steps.

Later that week the Personnel Director and the Superintendent meet to discuss the contents of the memo. The Superintendent generally favors the plan, but she wants the Personnel Director to delete the discussion of prospective counseling before the memo is circulated to the Board and the teachers' union. Although the Superintendent endorses the idea, she is uneasy about sharing this information with the union.

While the Board and the teachers' union debate the merits of the Personnel Director's proposal, he proceeds with the selection of the six teachers who will be added to the district's teaching staff. The Personnel Director invites twelve applicants to participate in the final screening and arranges for each of them to present a demonstration lesson before the selection panel. The panel selects six of the finalists; the choices are unanimous.

Meanwhile back at the bargaining table, the Board and the teachers' union agree to adopt a modified version of the Personnel Director's plan. Although the Board recognizes that principals will need to increase the time devoted to evaluating probationary teachers, it is unwilling to authorize a reduction in the frequency with which tenured teachers are evaluated. The Board also questions the wisdom of using self-evaluations as part of the tenure review process and rejects this aspect of the plan. The teachers' union objects to several features of the proposal as well. As a result of these objections, student ratings are not used to evaluate probationary teachers and eligibility for the three teacher assistance plans (PDP, IAP and EAP) is broadened to include tenured teachers. A non-profit educational foundation is formed to provide financial support for the teacher assistance plans and the in-service training program for principals.

As a time conservation measure, each of the six teachers is assigned to a different principal. The principals spend considerable time in the classrooms of these teachers and in conferring with them about their performance.[4] Five of the teachers experience some difficulties in the classroom, and their principals are forthright in pointing out these weaknesses and problems. All of these teachers choose to participate in the Professional Development and Instructional Assistance Programs. By the end of the probationary period, two of these teachers have shown marked improvement and are recommended for tenure. The one teacher who has performed satisfactorily throughout the entire probationary period is also recommended for tenure by the Principal and the Tenure Committee. The three teachers who have been denied tenure receive help through the Employee Assistance Program in making the transition to other lines of work. One of these teachers decides to look for another teaching position before seeking employment outside the field of education.

Post-Tenure

Several years pass. One of the teachers resigns to pursue a more lucrative career. Another begins to experience difficulties in the classroom which stem from problems at home. This teacher is going through a divorce, and she is unable to cope with it. She requests help through the Employee Assistance Program, and within three months she has pieced her personal life back together. She, like the third member of her cohort, is now doing a fine job in the classroom.

This pattern repeats itself over the next few years. Many teachers are hired, but only half of them are granted tenure. Some of these later leave for greener pastures. Fifteen years after the introduction of the new tenure policy only 58 per cent of the entire teaching staff is on tenure. The district has been successful on two counts: (a) it has retained institutional flexibility; and (b) it has little, if any, deadwood on the teaching staff.

Faced with the prospects of another period of declining enrollments and budget cutbacks, the Personnel Director sits back in his chair and reflects on what is happening. He is grateful for the foresight of his predecessor who retired three years ago. Because of his forward planning and stringent tenure policy, the district has not found it necessary to use escape hatches to sidestep the problems posed by incompetent tenured teachers. Administrators also have been spared countless hours in trying to salvage veteran teachers who should never have been hired in the first place. Moreover, the district will be able to avoid the pain and agony of its neighbors. There will be no need to issue layoff notices and little or no need to pressure senior members of the teaching staff to resign or to retire early. Since some of the tactics which are being used to obtain resignations run against his moral grain, he prefers to be in a position where the district does not replace teachers who leave voluntarily or who fail to meet the standards for tenure. Finally, there is even the possibility that the district may be able to raise its standards for permanent employment; henceforth, only exceptional teachers may be granted tenure. Thanks to the foresight of his predecessor, the forthcoming period of retrenchment presents an opportunity, not a crisis, for the district. Fortunately, history has not repeated itself.

Summary and Conclusion

Nearly 400,000 new teachers will be hired in the public schools during the decade of the 1990s. This influx provides school districts with an opportunity to upgrade the quality of their teachers for future generations of students. In an effort to foreshadow how school districts might respond to this opportunity, I have painted two scenarios entitled the *The Perils* and *The Possibilities*.[5]

The first scenario, *The Perils*, is patterned after the events described in chapters 2, 3 and 4. In this scenario, many teachers are hired in a relatively brief time span during a period of teacher scarcity. These teachers, including the weak ones, are not closely supervised during their probationary period and are given the benefit-of-the-doubt when the tenure decision is made. Their personnel records are filled with glowing generalities, double-talk, and inflated ratings. When problems later arise which cannot be ignored, administrators rely on escape hatches to sidestep or minimize the troubles created by the incompetent teachers. This response suffices until enrollments begin to fall and the district experiences a financial squeeze. At that point the incompetent teachers are returned to regular classroom teaching assignments. Parents complain about their children being shortchanged by these teachers. These complaints trigger abortive salvage attempts which eventually result in efforts by administrators to secure a resignation or an early retirement. In this scenario the influx of new teachers represents a lost opportunity and a repetition of history.

The second scenario, *The Possibilities*, contains a proposal which seeks to avoid the problems of the past and to capitalize on the opportunity presented by hiring large numbers of new teachers. This proposal draws heavily on the research that we have conducted, as well as a review of the literature that bears on the problems of poor performance and tenure. The policies and practices contained in this proposal attempt to deal constructively with the organizational realities faced by most school districts. Some of these realities relate to the legal obstacles and financial burdens associated with dismissing tenured teachers, the indeterminacy inherent in teacher evaluation, the scarcity of time and other resources, the problematic effectiveness of remediation with veteran teachers, and the changing fortunes of organizational life. The key elements of this proposal are as follows: (i) the concentration of scarce resources on the selection, evaluation, and development of probationary teachers; (ii) the use of institutional need, as well as individual merit, in deciding whether teachers are granted tenure; (iii) the adoption of more stringent procedures for awarding tenure; and (iv) the provision of outplacement counseling for those teachers who fail to receive tenure.

If these two scenarios inspire administrators, Board members, and teachers to reflect on their own local personnel policies and practices and to institute changes which alleviate the problem of teacher incompetence, the purposes for this book will have been accomplished. For, 'one seeks "pre-vision" as much to "halt" a future as help it come into being' (Bell, 1964).

Notes

1 Some common rationalizations or excuses which are currently being used by administrators to justify inaction are as follows: (i) 'It's too costly'; (ii) 'You can never win'; and (iii) 'It's too time consuming'. For ways of combatting these rationalizations see Bridges and Groves (1984).
2 A new principal may mean trouble for the incompetent teacher. In some contexts everybody comes to accept a person's shortcomings and adjust to them, especially if the person has some strengths. A change of principals may upset the equilibrium, and (s)he may be less forgiving or understanding. If parents complain, the new principal may be even more likely to move against the incompetent teacher.

3 For the reader who wishes to read further about some of the ideas contained in this memo, we will suggest additional references. Rather than sprinkle footnotes throughout the memo, we have chosen to cite the references in relation to the topics treated in it. Although this approach may represent a bit of inconvenience for the reader, we felt that the placement of footnotes in the memo would detract from its authenticity because inter-office communications do not ordinarily contain footnotes and references.

(a) *Teacher selection*

Two of these methods are currently being used by a few districts in California. Nearly nine per cent of the 141 districts participating in the statewide survey reported that they required demonstration lessons as a part of the selection process; another 49 per cent indicated that they may use this method in the future. Video-tapes of lessons presented during student teaching were used much less frequently (0.7 per cent); however, 46 per cent of the districts indicated that this method was under consideration.

(b) *Importance of the tenure decision*

For a useful discussion of the strengths and weaknesses of alternatives to tenure, see Chait and Ford (1982). Although this book treats tenure in higher education, the analysis and the research results should be of value and interest to policy makers in elementary and secondary education. We could locate no comparable work on tenure at the lower levels of education.

(c) *Hard on the standards*

The statement on the meaning of the term, 'preponderance of the evidence', is taken from Phay (1982), p. 62.

According to Louis M. Smith, school officials in the Clayton, Missouri, School District refer to the flair factor as 'second suits'. These second suits are the things a teacher can and likes to do with students beyond what is expected of the regular classroom teacher. Districts which require teachers to possess a flair factor or a second suit are striving to use excellence, rather than competence, as a standard for judging teaching performance.

(d) *Soft on the people*

See Lortie (1975) for an insightful discussion and analysis of the weaknesses inherent in the socialization experiences of teachers. The dynamics of job loss are treated in Brammer and Humberger (1984) and Kaufman (1982). Both of these books deal with the personal and career problems engendered by job loss and offer constructive suggestions for helping people cope with these problems.

(e) *Commitment from the top*

This commitment is a necessary ingredient of any effort to upgrade the quality of teaching; without this commitment the efforts are destined to fail. Two of the ways in which the Board and Superintendent can demonstrate their commitment are as follows: (i) exhibit a concern for the role of trade-offs in collective bargaining and adopt priorities which reflect the district's commitment to quality instruction; and (ii) allocate the financial resources needed to implement the elements of a strong teacher evaluation program (for example, inservice education for principals and remedial assistance for teachers). See Bridges and Groves (1990) for a discussion of the various techniques which can be used to heighten a district's concern for competent classroom performance.

(f) *Defensible criteria*
Medley *et al.* (1984) review the research on teacher effectiveness and provide educators with direct access to the findings of this body of research. Moreover, these researchers indicate whether the behaviors are effective across particular grade levels, various socioeconomic levels of students, and outcomes (reading achievement, arithmetic achievement and attitudes toward self and school).

(g) *Multiple sources of evidence*
For a review of the research on the soundness and legal defensibility of various types of informational sources, see Bridges and Groves (1990). The authors review what is known about the soundness of these different types of information in promoting teacher improvement and in measuring overall teacher effectiveness.

(h) *Staff development*
See Wise *et al.* (1984) for a description of practices which are currently being used by school districts to foster teacher growth and development. This research report reviews practices of four school districts that have exemplary programs.

(i) *Personal assistance*
Hosokawa and Thoreson (1984) provide a comprehensive view of employee assistance programs in higher education.

(j) *Evaluator competence*
The proficiency of evaluators is problematic in most districts and warrants special attention. See Bridges and Groves (1990) for a discussion of a multifaceted approach to this vexatious problem. They identify the requisite competencies and discuss three types of competency assurance programs that are being used by some local school districts.

(k) *Sufficient resources*
If supervisors are to fulfill their responsibilities for evaluating the instructional staff, they need a variety of resources. Specifically, supervisors need time, authority, access to remedial assistance, access to legal counsel, and support. Without these particular resources supervisors are unlikely to meet the organization's expectations even if they are committed to performing the appraisal function effectively and have the requisite skills and knowledge. Supervisory effort and ability are necessary but insufficient conditions for effective performance appraisal; organizational resources also play a crucial role in the process of evaluating teachers. See Bridges and Groves (1990) for a discussion of these various resources.

(l) *Principal accountability*
Most school districts do not hold principals accountable for evaluating teachers and working with those who are in difficulty (Groves, 1985). Districts which wish to hold principals accountable should adopt and

enforce policies which (i) discourage supervisors from inflating the evaluations of incompetent teachers; (ii) counter the tendencies of supervisors to postpone dealing with an incompetent teacher and to use rationalizations which bolster their procrastination; (iii) discourage supervisors from passing the poor performer to someone else in the district; and (iv) encourage principals to provide instructional leadership. See Bridges and Groves (1990) for examples of such policies.

(m) *Faculty staffing plan*

Chait and Ford (1982) provide numerous examples of this practice among institutions of higher education. A simple way to begin is with an inventory of teacher resources within the district. A data base might be developed which contains the following information about each teacher: Date of initial appointment, tenure status (date awarded tenure or tenure decision due), grade level(s) taught, subjects certified to teach, age, mandatory retirement date, sex, race, and current salary. This information can be used to provide annual answers to questions like the following: What proportion of our teaching staff has tenure? What proportion of our staff has tenure by level taught (elementary and high school), subject matter area (math, English, science, etc.), sex, and racial group? How many mandatory retirements will occur in each of the next five years? Based on recent trends, what is the probability of voluntary retirement at age 55? 60? 65? On the average, what percentage of the teaching staff, by tenure status, departs voluntarily? On the average, what per cent of the probationary teachers do not earn appointment to tenure? What proportion of the current operating budget goes for the salaries of tenured and non-tenured teachers? What proportion of the operating budget will go for the salaries of tenured and non-tenured teachers for each of the next five years?

(n) *Less attention to the evaluation and development of our tenured teachers*

The beneficial effects of teacher evaluation and the imposition of sanctions are reported in Natriello (1984) and Groves (1985). The results of Groves' study are consistent with the findings of O'Reilly (1980) who found that productivity in private business was enhanced by using negative sanctions against marginal employees. Groves discovered that student achievement in reading was positively associated with the number of sanctions imposed by principals against incompetent teachers.

(o) *More errors in denying tenure*

One way of avoiding these errors is to have a relatively long probationary period, perhaps five to seven years. A two-year probationary period does not seem to provide sufficient time for the teacher who is having some difficulties in the classroom but showing improvement to demonstate that s(he) is capable of becoming a fully satisfactory teacher.

(p) *More money*

For a comprehensive discussion of public educational foundations, see Clay *et al.* (1985). This monograph describes the procedures for setting up a public school foundation, the legal and tax aspects of these foundations, and the various ways to raise money through this mechanism. The fund-raising activities which they describe can be used in a range of socioeconomic settings.

4 The principal serves as the primary evaluator in the teacher evaluation plan outlined in this chapter. In Toledo, Ohio, teachers serve in this capacity and have shown a willingness to deny probationary teachers tenure. See Wise *et al.* (1984) for a description and analysis of the Toledo plan.

5 I am indebted to Lee Shulman for stimulating me to consider the use of scenarios in framing this chapter.

Chapter 8

Promoting Teacher Quality: Further Reflections

Since the initial publication of this book, I have continued to reflect on the problem of teacher incompetence and to re-examine my views on this important, but controversial, issue. In this final chapter I want to share with the reader my current thoughts about five interrelated policy issues: (1) the possibilities and the prospects for improving the selection process; (2) the need to improve the ways in which teachers are treated during the early stages of their career; (3) the meaning of 'fully competent' performance as the basis for awarding tenure; (4) the standard of performance which is appropriate for revoking tenure; and (5) the importance of designing educational organizations which encourage educators to own, rather than deny or sidestep, the problem of incompetence. These five issues, in my judgment, form the core of any concerted effort to obtain and maintain a teaching force that is capable of meeting the challenges which lie ahead.

Selection

My views on selection have changed substantially since this book was first published. At that time I equated selection with hiring; I now view selection as the tenure decision and hiring as an investigatory decision. Moreover, my views on the hiring process have also been revised. Reading the research and literature on personnel decisions produced these shifts.

In Chapter 6 I underscored the importance of making sound selection decisions. Like most writers on the subject, I emphasized ways in which school districts might obtain valid information about applicants for teaching positions during the hiring process. Retrospectively, I realize that this perspective on the problem was myopic.

School districts wish to predict how applicants are likely to behave in particular contexts. When making hiring decisions, districts should consider two types of information: (1) information about the candidate's behavior and (2) information about the context in which this behavior has been and will be exhibited. A district can expect to make more accurate predictions if it observes an applicant's behavior in a context that is maximally similar to the one in which he will later perform. By way of example, the district, as part of the hiring process, should observe applicants teaching students in a setting maximally similar to the one for which they are being hired. If the applicant is expected to teach two different types of classes (e.g., English for college-bound and remedial students), the candidate should be observed in both situations. For those applicants who have previous experience but cannot be observed by district officials, information should be gathered about the nature of the candidate's previous teaching assignments and his performance in each of these assignments.

To my knowledge, no school district explicitly collects information about the context in which a candidate has taught and uses this information in making hiring decisions. The shortsightedness of this approach became apparent to me when I was working with a local school district that was interested in learning from its hiring mistakes. The first teacher whom we examined had a superb evaluation from her student teaching supervisor. The supervisor maintained that the person was the strongest student teacher he had worked with in twenty-five years; he documented this assertion extensively. This reference, confirmed by phone, played a crucial role in the district's hiring decision. Throughout the year the teacher was an excellent performer with the students in her advanced math classes; however, she was a disaster with students in basic and general math. As we studied the teacher's employment file, we discovered that the student teaching supervisor had observed the student in only one type of setting — advanced math. His evaluation accurately predicted the student's teaching performance in a similar context. Alas, the district needed the teacher to perform in different contexts, and she was unable to do it even with assistance. Perhaps districts can improve their ratio of hits to misses by describing the context(s) in which the person will be expected to perform and then seeking to gather information about the behavior of applicants in these various contexts. The axiom, 'Past behavior is the best predictor of future behavior', should be amended to read, 'Past behavior is the best predictor of future behavior when the contexts are similar'. This 'behavior-context consistency' view of selection now figures prominently in my thinking about the subject.

Although I earnestly believe that school districts can pick more winners and fewer losers by using the 'behavior-context consistency' approach to hiring teachers, I, paradoxically, am less optimistic than I was about a district's capacity to predict the quality of a person's teaching performance. My diminished optimism stems from reading reviews of the research on the validity and fairness of employee selection procedures (Ghiselli, 1973; Reilly and Chao, 1982; Schmitt *et al.*, 1984). Reilly and Chao (1982) reviewed the research on eight different alternatives to the use of paper-and-pencil tests. Like other reviewers, they found that interviews, self-assessments, reference checks, academic achievement, expert judgment, and projective techniques had levels of validity generally below those reported for paper-and-pencil tests. Only biodata and peer evaluation had validities substantially equal to those for standardized tests. Given the relatively low validity coefficients for these tests (.35 when using proficiency criteria; see Ghiselli, 1973), there is little reason to expect that school officials will achieve better results for a complex job like teaching even when the contexts are taken into account.

In light of these results across a range of jobs, occupations, and selection procedures, I now believe that it makes more sense to view the initial hiring decision as an *investigatory decision*, not as a selection decision. When other factors are considered, this altered view seems even more plausible. Colleges and universities do not perform their screening function well, nor do they generally prepare teachers fully to cope with the realities of classroom teaching. Moreover, the scholastic aptitude test scores of individuals who are electing teaching as a career have dropped in recent years (Kerr, 1983), and the prospects for reversing this trend are slim. It is unlikely that the prestige and salaries of teachers, relative to other occupations, will change dramatically. In short, there are reasonable grounds for questioning the ability of some newcomers 'to stand and deliver'.

When the hiring decision is viewed as an investigatory decision, it merely represents a decision to obtain additional information about the individual's performance once he has been hired. In effect, the district is saying,

> Based on the information which we now have, we think your potential is promising enough that we intend to give you an opportunity to prove yourself in our district. We also intend

to create conditions where your potential can be realized. However, there is always the possibility that we have mis-gauged your potential. In this event, you will not be granted tenure. Unfortunately, our hiring process is not fool-proof.

Treatment of New Hires

During the past two years, I have come to appreciate more fully that competent performance is primarily a function of three factors: (1) the level of demands inherent in a teacher's assignment; (2) the organizational resources which a teacher has to meet these demands; and (3) the personal resources which the teacher brings to the role. Since all three of these factors are problematic for beginning teachers, I now recognize how important it is for school districts to create conditions which are more conducive to becoming a fully competent teacher. In line with this view, the probationary period should be a time for beginners to improve, as well as prove, their competence. Moreover, they should prove themselves in assignments which represent a reasonable level of difficulty in terms of organizational demands and resources.

Compared with veteran teachers, beginners often face greater demands and have fewer organizational resources. They typically are assigned more of everything — more preparations, more extra-curricular duties, more students who are viewed as tough to teach (e.g., behavior problems, learners with special needs, and limited English speaking), and more locations (rooms or buildings) in which to teach. Although beginning teachers generally face more challenging assignments, they are likely to possess fewer organizational resources to meet these demands. When teachers resign or retire, the veterans, not the beginners, inherit the supplies, materials, and equipment from those who have left. Veteran teachers also have accumulated numerous resources over the years through their own efforts. Unless these veterans share their 'wealth', the newcomers are apt to be resource poor relative to their senior colleagues.

Even if beginners received adequate resources and assignments with a reasonable level of difficulty, their capacity to deliver a competent classroom performance is problematic. Beginners commonly lack the personal resources and skills to handle the complexities of teaching. When they graduate from college, they are not finished products; they are burgeoning professionals who require substantive and emotional support to develop their own inner resources. Without this support, the beginner's growth as a competent professional may be temporarily thwarted or permanently and irreversibly stunded. Regrettably, such support is the exception; 'sink or swim' is the rule (Lortie, 1977).

The combination of fewer resources and a more demanding work assignment is not conducive to improving or proving oneself as a fully competent teacher. If this situation is to be redressed, administrators and veteran teachers must share the responsibility. Organizational resources are relatively fixed and scarce; they are unlikely to be committed to beginning teachers unless teachers and administrators agree to the reallocation. Creating more reasonable teaching assignments for beginners also poses a challenge to educators. Teaching assignments profoundly influence two critical aspects of a teacher's work life — the psychic rewards and the level of effort. Providing beginning teachers with less demanding teaching assignments may mean diminished psychic rewards and increased effort for veteran teachers. In such instances, changes are likely to occur only if the veterans on the teaching staff are willing to assume a more difficult teaching assignment. There are grounds for optimism because teachers in some schools have already exhibited the strong sense of professionalism needed to make this sacrifice (Szabo, 1990).

Granting Tenure

My views on the granting of tenure have changed. In Chapter 7, speaking through a memo written by a hypothetical personnel director, I argued two main points. First, tenure should not be automatic the way it often is now; rather, tenure should be granted only if there is ample evidence to substantiate the claim that the teacher is worthy of tenure. Second, tenure should be granted to those who are 'fully competent'. By fully competent, I meant that the person satisfied the criteria which are used to evaluate teachers and possess at least one quality (a flair factor) which sets him apart from most of the teachers already on the teaching staff. This flair factor might be special talents in art or music, ability to work with students from different ethnic and racial backgrounds, or working knowledge of another language or culture. I continue to believe that tenure should not be granted unless the preponderance of the evidence elicits a reasonable belief that the teacher is fully competent. However, I have changed my views on what it means to be fully competent.

Fully competent should mean that the teacher has demonstrated *in multiple contexts* his ability to satisfy the criteria which are used to evaluate teachers. These contexts should be differentiated primarily on the ability, ethnic status, and socio-economic status of students. If districts use this definition of 'fully competent', they need to evaluate the performance of the probationary teacher in different teaching assignments. No teacher should be granted tenure unless he demonstrates that he is competent in teaching the full range of students represented in the district (excluding those who have severe learning disabilities or handicaps). If the teacher is unable to cope effectively with this diversity, he should be denied tenure unless he is truly gifted in teaching a particular type of student.

My reasons for re-defining the meaning of fully competent stem in part from my subsequent reflections on how administrators deal with tenured teachers who are incompetent. As I pointed out in Chapter 2, some administrators use various escape hatches to skirt the problems created by incompetent teachers. One of these escape hatches is reassignment of such teachers to a school or a class which is attended primarily by students from educationally, socially, or economically disadvantaged backgrounds. This questionable practice violates the Fourteenth Amendment of the US Constitution. Passed shortly after the Civil War, this amendment aspired to grant equal protection and due process to the newly freed slaves. Ironically, more than a century later, teachers have acquired the rights to due process, and these rights have contributed indirectly to the denial of equal protection and educational opportunities for students from disadvantaged backgrounds. Once teachers receive tenure and begin to manifest performance problems, disadvantaged students may become the victims of a complaint-driven approach to teacher evaluation. They should not be shortchanged because their parents are less likely to complain than the parents of middle-class students. By insisting on the competence of teachers to teach the full range of students prior to being granted tenure, districts lessen the probability that students of any race, creed, color, or ability will be cheated.

I have also been influenced by two societal trends. Increasingly, students who attend the public schools are being drawn from non-white and non-middle class backgrounds. In California, for example, the minorities have become the majority. This trend, when combined with the historic inability of schools to close the achievement gap between students of differing social, economic, and ethnic backgrounds, augers serious problems ahead. It is imperative for the future welfare and stability of our society that students from these backgrounds receive fully competent instruction. My revised notion of what it means to be fully competent in relation to tenure reflects a concern for societal stability, as well as social justice and educational equity.

Revoking Tenure

The standard of performance for determining whether there is cause for dismissing a tenured teacher is set much too low. Incompetence has come to mean blatant failure in performing one's duties. Students have an interest in and a right to a quality education because it exerts a profound effect on their future life chances. To presume, as we do now, that the teacher's employment interests override the students' interest in a quality education unless there is egregious failure is indefensible. We need to adopt a standard for revoking tenure that restores the balance between these potentially competing interests. This standard is marginal performance, not incompetence.

By marginal performance I mean that *the person's performance falls just short of fulfilling one or more of the professional duties of a teacher.* The local board, in consultation or negotiations with the teachers' association, should determine what these duties are. Scriven's (1988) list of professional duties provides a worthwhile starting point for these discussions:

1 Know the subject matter;
2 Design instruction;
3 Select and create materials;
4 Construct tests;
5 Grade or mark students' performance;
6 Provide information to students about their achievements;
7 Provide information to administration;
8 Provide information to parents, guardians, and authorities;
9 Use resources;
10 Communicate effectively;
11 Manage the classroom;
12 Engage in self-evaluation and development;
13 Render service to the profession; and
14 Acquire and use knowledge of the school and community.

When attempting to demonstrate that a teacher is a marginal performer, a school district would have a two-fold obligation: (1) offer a reasonable basis for the judgment that students are not receiving a quality education from the teacher and (2) provide evidence to substantiate its claim that the teacher's performance falls just short of fulfilling one or more of his/her professional duties. If state legislatures replace incompetence with marginal performance as grounds for dismissal, administrators can hold tenured teachers accountable for a higher and more reasonable standard of performance than now exists. Moreover, since marginal performance is easier to prove than incompetence, administrators are apt to be more willing to confront teachers who are shortchanging students in the classroom.

In addition to revising the standard for revoking tenure, state legislatures should curtail the opportunities to appeal dismissal decisions. There should be no appeals for decisions made by a hearing officer, Commission on Professional Competence, or other impartial third party not directly affiliated with the district. Binding arbitration works well for resolving disputes over collective bargaining agreements; the decision of the arbitrator is final and unappealable.

Tenured teachers should receive due process; however, they, as well as school districts, should have only one bite at the apple. The tenured teacher deserves to be protected against arbitrary and unreasonable treatment; proceedings conducted by an impartial third party who has no direct stake in the outcome serve this purpose well.

The Centrality of Problem Ownership

In retrospect, my initial analysis underestimated the significance of one variable — owning the problem. Based on my research, I knew that administrators were reluctant to confront poor performers and that teachers reacted defensively when they were confronted. What I did not fully appreciate was how the responses of both teachers and administrators reflected a failure to own the problem. Nor did I realize how resistant people are to owning their problems and doing something about them. These insights emerged from reading two quite different books, *High Output Management* (Grove, 1983) and *The Road Less Traveled* (Peck, 1978).

The most common responses of administrators and teachers to the problem of incompetence are summarized in *Figure 1* below. This figure highlights the reluctance of administrators and incompetent

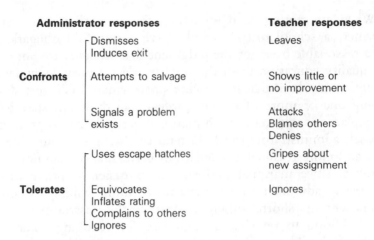

Figure 1: *Parallels between administrator and teacher responses to the problem of teacher incompetence.*

teachers to own the problem. Administrators are inclined to tolerate the poor performance and rarely confront the incompetent teacher. Incompetent teachers, once confronted, deny, blame others for their difficulties, and even attack the sources of the criticism. They do not own the problem; nor do they assume responsibility for solving it. The reluctance of administrators and teachers to own the problem probably accounts in large part for the persistence of the problem in the schools and the unsuccessful efforts to deal with it.

Why are teachers, as well as administrators, reluctant to own the problem? The reasons which I offered in Chapter 2 may partially account for it. The ambiguities inherent in teacher evaluation simply may create a situation which makes any supervisor's judgment lack credibility. If the evaluation is not judged credible, the evaluatee perceives that no problem exists and, therefore, sees no compelling reason to own it. An understandable reaction by the teacher under these conditions would be, 'The supervisor must have it in for me'. There is also the possibility that the teacher's legal protections may foster a feeling of quasi-invincibility. The teacher may feel the same way as the administrator, 'It's virtually impossible to get rid of a tenured teacher for incompetence'. Dismissal is considered to be such a remote possibility that the teacher never takes the problem seriously. Since I have not interviewed teachers who were dismissed or induced to leave, I do not know whether either explanation applies.

An explanation that currently appeals to me is the one offered by Peck (1978), a psychiatrist. In *The Road Less Traveled*, he convincingly argues that people from all walks of life will go to ridiculous extremes to avoid assuming responsibility for their problems and their solution. He vividly makes this point with numerous cases drawn from his own professional practice.

Peck's view, admittedly based on his experiences with troubled individuals, coincides with Grove's (1983) analysis of the breakdowns which occur in solving organizational problems. According to Grove, the problem-solving process proceeds through five steps: ignore, deny, blame others, assume responsibility, and find a solution. He maintains that the process gets stuck at the blame-others stage. If the individual is able to make the transition from blaming others to assuming responsibility, finding the solution is relatively easy because it is an intellectual, rather than an emotional, step. Unfortunately, Grove, like Peck, provides no insight into the organizational conditions which nurture or thwart problem ownership.

After years of wrestling with the problem of teacher incompetence, I now consider that the fundamental question is, 'How do we create organizational environments in which people *willingly* own, rather than deny or sidestep, performance problems?' My own thoughts on this basic question suggest some possible approaches, but no guarantees. I sense that creating a climate for owning and solving performance problems represents a formidable challenge for scholars and practitioners alike.

When thinking about the organizational conditions which are conducive to problem ownership, I believe that it is essential to distinguish between problems that are disclosed by the teachers themselves and those brought to light by their supervisors. In designing an organizational climate that encourages problem ownership, one approach is to reward, rather than punish, problem disclosure by teachers. If one of the professional duties of a teacher is self-evaluation and development, teachers who come forward with their problems and seek help in solving them should be judged positively, not negatively, for their actions. When a teacher discloses that she is having problems and needs help, the supervisor should not foist a solution on the teacher unless there clearly is a predetermined answer to the teacher's problem. Rather, the supervisor should adopt a problem-centered orientation that assists the teacher in exploring and clarifying his own thoughts and feelings about the problem and its possible solutions. If the teacher is unable to implement one or more of the solutions without assistance, the supervisor should seek to provide what the teacher needs.

In those instances where the teacher is unaware of the problem or is aware but doing nothing about it, the supervisor is obligated to initiate discussion of the performance problem. When it becomes necessary for the supervisor to act, he could place emphasis on posing the problem, not prescribing a solution. The problem can be posed in different ways depending upon its nature. According to Margerison (1974), posing the problem in personal terms is far more likely to evoke a defensive reaction from the teacher than one which is posed in situational terms. For example, the supervisor may be flooded with complaints about a teacher and parental requests to have their children transferred to another class. Faced with this problem, the supervisor can personalize the posing of the problem by saying something like, 'Numerous parents have expressed dissatisfaction with your teaching, and in my judgment their complaints are warranted. You spend too much time on discipline and too little time on instruction'. Alternately, the supervisor may pose the problem in situational terms by saying, 'In the past two days I have received six letters of complaint from parents about your teaching and seven parental requests to have their children transferred out of your classroom. These parents are obviously disgruntled and expect me to do something. What are your thoughts and feelings about this matter?' By describing the situation and asking the question, the supervisor seeks to set the stage for helping the teacher to explore his feelings, clarify his own views of the problem, and to consider possible solutions. In this way, the supervisor maximizes his chances of becoming a helper rather than an adversary.

Summary

In this final chapter I have discussed my current thinking on five interrelated policy issues: selection, treatment of beginning teachers, granting tenure, revoking tenure, and creating organizations which encourage problem ownership. I now believe that our success in obtaining a quality teaching force depends in large part on how we think about and resolve these five issues. My afterthoughts on these issues are summarized below:

Selection

To increase the odds of picking a winner, districts should adopt a 'behavior-context consistency' approach. That is, they should gather two types of information prior to making the hiring decision: (1) information about the behavior of the individual, especially behavior that closely corresponds to the behavior expected on the job, and (2) information about the context in which the behavior has been and will be exhibited. A district can expect to make more accurate predictions if it observes an applicant's behavior in a context that corresponds to the one in which he will later perform.

Although the 'behavior-context consistency' approach to hiring may improve the ratio of hits to misses, mistakes are inevitable. There are no fool-proof methods for distinguishing the winners from the losers in the hiring process. Accordingly, a district should view the hiring decision as an *investigatory decision* (i.e., a decision to gather more information about the candidate after he has been hired) and tenure as the selection decision.

Treatment of beginners

School districts should create conditions for beginning teachers which are more conducive to becoming a fully competent teacher. The practice of assigning beginners more of everything (more preparations, more students who are viewed as tough to teach, and more locations in which to teach) should be abandoned. Moreover, districts should provide the organizational resources which the beginner needs in order to meet the demands inherent in his role and should offer opportunities for the beginner to develop his own inner resources. In short, probation should be viewed as a time for beginners to improve, as well as prove, their competence under conditions that are much more likely to produce success than failure or frustration.

Granting tenure

Tenure should be earned. Teachers should receive tenure only if there is compelling evidence that they are fully competent professionals. Fully competent means that the teacher is effective in multiple contexts, contexts defined primarily in terms of the types of students being taught. If the district serves a diverse student body, the teacher should demonstrate his ability to handle this diversity effectively prior to being granted tenure. This definition of competence reflects a concern for social justice, educational equity, and societal stability.

Revoking tenure

The standard of performance for revoking tenure should be raised. Incompetence (blatant failure in the classroom) is much too low. It should be replaced with a standard that balances the interests of students in a quality education with the interests of a teacher in continued employment. This standard is marginal performance (i.e., the teacher's performance falls just short of fulfilling one or more of his professional duties). Moreover, when an impartial third party decides that there are grounds for dismissal, the decision should be final and binding. Neither the district nor the teacher should have more than one bite at the apple.

Owning the problem

Incompetence is education's shunted orphan. Few people exhibit much interest in assuming responsibility for the problem; as long as educators decline to own it, the problem won't be solved. The challenge for scholars and practitioners alike is to find an answer to this fundamental question, 'How do we create organizational environments in which people *willingly* own, rather than deny or sidestep, performance problems?'

When thinking about the answers to this basic question, it is important to distinguish between problems that are disclosed voluntarily by teachers and those which are brought to light by supervisors. Each point of origin affords a separate, but complementary, approach to this vexing issue. If one of the professional duties of a teacher is self-evaluation and development, teachers can be rewarded, rather than punished, for disclosing their problems and trying to solve them. In those instances where the teacher is unaware of the problem or is aware but doing nothing about it, the supervisor is obligated to take action. When discussing the problem with the teacher, the supervisor should initially centre on the problem, not the solution; moreover, he should attempt to pose the problem in situational, rather than personal, terms. By adopting these responses to performance problems, the administrator may stimulate poor performers to own their problems and find their own solutions.

The final chapter on problem ownership has yet to be written. I have framed the question, issued the challenge, and sketched two possible approaches to creating an organizational climate conducive to owning performance problems. Perhaps, these efforts will stimulate others to pursue the issue and to discover more satisfying answers. The person who succeeds deserves the everlasting gratitude of everyone who cares deeply about the quality of public education!

Appendix A. Interview Study

1 Purpose

The major purpose of the interview study was to obtain information about the events and circumstances surrounding the induced resignations and early retirements of incompetent teachers. Each interview produced a case history of an incompetent teacher who had recently been induced to leave the district.

2 Sample

Thirty school administrators (twenty-three directors of personnel, four superintendents, one elementary principal, one middle school principal and one high school principal) provided the information requested in the interview guide. Each of these administrators worked in different districts located throughout the state of California. These administrators constitute a sample of convenience rather a random sample. Each administrator had been involved in at least one induced departure over the past two years and expressed a willingness to talk about the circumstances surrounding the induced exit. We pledged to safeguard the anonymity of the administrator, the district, and the teacher.

To fulfill our obligation to these thirty school administrators who spoke openly and candidly about the ways in which they deal with incompetent teachers, we have chosen to characterize the districts in which they are employed in quite general terms. All thirty school districts are covered by a collective bargaining agreement. Most of the labor contracts have been negotiated with an affiliate of the California Teachers' Association (n = 27) and the remainder with the American

Federation of Teachers (n = 3). The districts range in size from approximately 600 students to almost 44,000 students; six districts have less than 5000 students while nine have more than 10,000. The other fifteen districts have between 5000 and 10,000 students. Most of the districts (n = 15) are unified school districts; i.e., contain grades K–12; three are high school districts; and the remainder (n = 12) are elementary school districts. Although the majority of these districts serve students who come predominantly from middle-class backgrounds, most of the districts have students from lower socio-economic status backgrounds as well. Four of the districts serve students drawn primarily from the lower class, and four serve students who come from the upper middle class. Approximately two-thirds of the districts have experienced declining enrollments during the past five years. Three districts are bucking the trend and are growing at the rate of 2 to 3 per cent annually while the other districts show a somewhat stable pattern of enrollment. Most, but not all, of these districts have experienced a serious financial squeeze in recent years.

3 Interview Guide

....
I.D. Code

Part A
(administered by phone)

1 Personal Information
    (a)   What is your official job title?
    (b)   How long have you served in this position?
    (c)   Briefly, what is your professional background?
2 District Information
    (a)   What is the enrollment of your district?
    (b)   How many full-time equivalent teachers are there in your district?
    (c)   Do the teachers in your district engage in collective bargaining?...... No
             ...... Yes (Ask: What organization represents them?)
3 Was it necessary to RIF (reduction in force) any teachers in your district last year?
    ....No

........Yes (Ask:

> How many of these teachers actually lost their jobs?
> ....
> Would you really like to re-hire this teacher?
> .... No
> > Why? ....
> .... Yes
> **OR**
> How many of these teachers would you really like to re-hire? .... Why?..........

4 How many of your teachers were given a 90-day notice for incompetency during the 1982–83 school year? ....

5 How many of your teachers were dismissed for cause during the 1982–83 school year? .... Any of these for incompetency? .... How many? ....

6 How many of your teachers have resigned or retired in the past two years? .... (If O, stop here: express appreciation.)

(a) Sometimes teachers resign because they are counseled out, are encouraged to take early retirement, are under pressure from the administration, or realize that their work is not appreciated. In other words, their resignations are not entirely voluntary. In your judgment,

How many of these resignations or retirements were not entirely voluntary? .... (If O, stop here; express appreciation.)

Did any of these resignations involve people whose classroom teaching was unsatisfactory?
.... No (Stop here; express appreciation.)
.... Yes (Ask:

> > Would it be possible for me to make an appointment with you in the near future to talk about *this teacher/one of these teachers* and the circumstances surrounding his/her resignation? Let me assure you that I will not ask you to disclose the name of this teacher and I will treat your comments in the strictest confidence.
> > .... No (Stop here; express appreciation.)
> > .... Yes (Ask:

Prefer morning or afternoon?

How about . . . .
on the . . . .?

I would appreciate it if you would review this teacher's personnel file before we meet and have it available when we talk. Look forward to
. . . .

Part B
(administered face-to-face)

7 When we spoke over the phone, you indicated that one of your teachers had resigned during the past two years and that this resignation was not entirely voluntary. Let's start out by my asking a few questions about the teacher.

(a) What did this teacher teach?
Grade level(s) . . . .
Subject(s) . . . .

(b) Was this teacher male . . . . . or female . . . . .?

(c) Was this teacher a minority? . . . . . Yes . . . . . No

(d) How old was this teacher? . . . .

(e) How long had this person taught in your district? . . . .

(f) Was this teacher active in the teacher's organization?
. . . . . Yes
. . . . . No

(g) To your knowledge, was this teacher generally liked by the other teachers? . . . . . Yes . . . . . No . . . . .?

8 You also indicated over the phone that this person's classroom teaching was unsatisfactory. What types of information indicated that this teacher was having difficulties in the classroom? (Hand list.)

. . . . . (a) Supervisor observations
. . . . . (b) Student ratings
. . . . . (c) Peer ratings
. . . . . (d) Complaints from other teachers

..... (e) Student test results
..... (f) Complaints from a Board member
..... (g) Student complaints
..... (h) Parent complaints
..... (i) Other

9 What was the nature of the teacher's difficulties in the classroom?

10 Which of these difficulties were the most serious?

11 What sorts of things may have contributed to the difficulties this teacher was having in the classroom? Here's a list of possibilities (hand to the person); let me know which seem to be applicable in this particular case. (Probe for specifics if the response is checked.)

..... (a) Difficult teaching assignment (for example, too many preparations, too many difficult students, too few resources)
..... (b) Shortcomings of the supervisor
..... (c) Lack of ability by the teacher
..... (d) Lack of effort or motivation by the teacher
..... (e) Personal disorder of the teacher (for example, alcoholism, drug use, mental illness, severe emotional distress, burned out.)
..... (f) Outside influences (for example, marital problems, financial difficulties, conflicts, or problems with children)
..... (g) Other:

If the respondent mentions two or more of the above, ask:
You mentioned (   ). Did these, in your judgment, contribute equally to this teacher's difficulties in the classroom, or was one of these more important than the other(s)?
..... Equally important
..... One more important (Ask: What was the most important one?)

12 How did the administration deal with this teacher in light of his/her difficulties? Here are a few possibilities. (Hand list to respondent.)

..... (a) Let the teacher know of his/her shortcomings.
Was a written record kept of these communications?
..... Yes (Ask: May I have a copy of these records if the names of personnel are inked out or eradicated? .....
If the person responds no, also ask question immediately below.)

..... No (Ask: How often was the teacher told?
How was the teacher told?)

..... (b) Provided the teacher with assistance.

Was a written record kept that describes the nature of the assistance which this teacher received?

..... Yes (Ask: May I have a copy of these records if the names of personnel are inked out or eradicated? ..... If the person responds no, also ask question immediately below.)

..... No (Ask: Could you give me some idea of the assistance which this teacher received? .... (Probe)

..... (c) Served the teacher with a 90-day notice. (If checked, ask: May I have a copy if names are inked out or eradicated? .....)

..... (d) Recommended the teacher for dismissal.

(e) SEE BELOW (if administration raised the possibility of a resignation).

or

(f) GO TO PAGE 156 (if teacher raised the possibility of a resignation).

..... (e) Administration raised the possibility of a resignation.

(1) Which of the following people were involved in making the decision to suggest a resignation? (Probe for nature of involvement. Hand list to respondent.)

..... Personnel Director
..... Principal
..... District Lawyer
..... Superintendent
..... Board of Education
..... Other

(2) Did any bargaining take place with the teacher in relation to the administration's suggestion of a resignation?

..... No

..... Yes (Ask: Which of the following people were involved at some point in the bargaining process? (Hand list. Probe for specifics.)

..... Personnel Director
..... Principal
..... Superintendent
..... Lawyer for district
..... Board of Education
..... Representative of teacher's organization
..... Teacher's lawyer
..... Teacher

(3) What sorts of things did the teacher request in exchange for the resignation?

(4) I'm interested in the final agreement that was reached between the teacher and the district.

Did the teacher receive anything from the district in return for the resignation?
..... No ..... Yes (Probe.)

What else did the teacher agree to do or not to do besides resign?

What did the administration agree to do or not to do in exchange for the resignation?

Were any steps taken to prevent the teacher from backing out of the agreement?
..... No ..... Yes (Probe.)

Were any steps taken to ensure that the administration would live up to its part of the agreement?
..... No ..... Yes (Probe.)

(5) Once the possibility of this resignation came up, how long did it take before the teacher submitted his/her resignation?
(SKIP TO PAGE 158)

..... (f) Teacher raised the possibility of a resignation and the administration eventually agreed to accept it.

(1) How was this possibility raised?

(2) What steps did the administration take that may have led the teacher to suggest a resignation?

(3) Which of the following people were involved in making the decision to accept the resignation? (Hand list to respondent; probe for nature of involvement.)

..... Personnel Director
..... Principal
..... District Lawyer
..... Superintendent
..... Board of Education
..... Other

(4) Did any bargaining take place with the teacher in relation to the possibility of a resignation?

..... No
..... Yes (Ask: Which of the following people were involved at some point in the bargaining process? Hand list. Probe for specifics.)

..... Personnel Director
..... Principal
..... Superintendent
..... Lawyer for district
..... Board of Education
..... Representative of teacher's organization
..... Teacher's lawyer
..... Teacher

(5) What sorts of things did the teacher request in exchange for the resignation?

(6) I'm interested in the final agreement that was reached between the teacher and the district.

Did the teacher receive anything from the district in return for the resignation?
..... No ..... Yes (Probe.)

What else did the teacher agree to do or not to do besides resign?

What did the administration agree to do or not to do in exchange for the resignation?

Were any steps taken to prevent the teacher from backing out of the agreement?
..... No ..... Yes (Probe.)

Were any steps taken to ensure that the administration would live up to its part of the agreement?
..... No :.... Yes (Probe.)

(7) Once the possibility of this resignation came up, how long did it take before the teacher submitted his/her resignation?

..... (g) Other (Probe.)

13 I wonder if we could shift our attention to the aftermath of this teacher's resignation.

(a) Did this teacher's resignation have any repercussions for the district or anyone in the district? ..... No ..... Yes (Probe)

(b) Do you have any sense of what has happened to this teacher? ..... No ..... Yes (Probe.)

(c) Was anyone hired to replace this teacher? ..... No ..... Yes (Probe. How well doing?)

(d) Do you have any second thoughts or regrets about the way the situation was handled or worked out? ..... No ..... Yes (Probe.)

(e) What advice would you give an administrator who may be thinking about getting involved in resignations of this type? (Probe.)

14 Finally, as you think about this particular case, is it typical of the resignations that are not entirely voluntary? ..... Yes ..... No (Probe.)

(In what ways is this resignation atypical?)

15 If you have any additional views on what is involved in dealing with incompetent teachers, we would appreciate hearing about them.

4 Data Analysis

The data from these thirty interviews were analyzed in two stages. First, the researchers used the notes taken during the interview to prepare a written report that detailed each administrator's response to the questions in the interview guide. Second, the researchers read and reread each of the thirty reports with the objective of identifying the various ways in which administrators respond to the incompetent teacher and the conditions or events which seem to shape their responses. This process continued until a pattern of relationships emerged which seemed to describe and to account for what was happening.

To check the validity of our analysis, we took several steps. First, we asked a principal, a personnel director, and three superintendents to review a draft of the book. This reality check, along with oral presentations of our findings to a group of superintendents and a group of personnel directors, indicated that our conclusions were consistent with their experiences. As a further check on the validity of our analysis, we conducted a statewide survey; the contents and results of this survey are described in Appendix B.

Appendix B. Mailed Survey

1 Purpose

The survey was designed to obtain information about the practices used by California school districts in dealing with incompetent teachers and to provide a partial test of the model presented in Chapter 2.

2 Sample

The survey was mailed to the superintendents or personnel directors of 150 school districts. These districts were drawn at random from the 581 districts in California which (a) enroll between 250 and 50,000 students; (b) contain at least two schools; and (c) have a full-time superintendent. Ninety-four per cent (n = 141) of the districts returned the questionnaire.

3 Questionnaire

To ensure a high rate of participation in the mailed survey, we used the Total Design Method recommended by Dillman (1978). The contents of the questionnaire, along with the results in parentheses, are reproduced below.

How School Districts Deal
with Incompetent Teachers

This survey is part of a study designed to help California school districts improve the ways in which they deal with incompetent teachers. Obtaining information about the practices of school districts is an important part of this study. All of the practices listed in this questionnaire have been used by one or more of the thirty school districts that we interviewed during an earlier phase of our project. We need to know if your district currently uses any of these practices or if it may use them in the future.

In order to have an accurate picture of what is happening throughout the state, we need to have a high rate of participation. The number stamped at the top of the questionnaire allows us to keep track of the people who have participated in the study. Neither your name nor the name of your district will ever be placed on this questionnaire or listed as a participant in any publications.

Instructions

1   Please answer the questions in order.

2   Most of the questions can be answered by circling the number which corresponds to your answer. Since some of the numbers are close together, please make sure that you only circle one number when you answer a question.

3   Please answer all of the questions. This is very important to our gaining a full and accurate picture of what is taking place in districts throughout the state. If you feel, however, that you don't want to answer a particular question, you are free to leave it blank.

4   Feel free to write in any reactions which you may have to the practices described in the questionnaire. Your comments will be read and taken into account.

5   Remember, the answers you give will be completely confidential.

6   When you have completed this questionnaire, please return it in the stamped, pre-addressed envelope we have provided to:

Project on Improving Teacher Quality
Stanford University
School of Education
Stanford, CA 94305

To begin, we would like to ask you some questions about your hiring practices, especially those practices which have been instituted to reduce the problems associated with hiring incompetent teachers.

Hiring

In the course of our research, we have discovered two practices which some districts are using to minimize mistakes at the selection stage. We are interested in knowing whether your district uses either of these practices.

1   Some districts require inexperienced applicants to submit video-tapes of themselves presenting a lesson during their student teaching. Does your district ever use this practice? [circle number]

   1   No and we are unlikely to use this practice (53.2 per cent)
   2   No but we may use this practice in the future (46.1 per cent)
   3   Yes (0.7 per cent)

2   Some districts require applicants for teaching positions to prepare a lesson based on an objective formulated by the selection committee. Applicants then teach the lesson to a small group of students while being observed by one or more members of the selection committee. Does your district ever use this practice? [circle number]

   1   No and we are unlikely to use this practice (42.1 per cent)
   2   No but we may use this practice in the future (49.3 per cent)
   3   Yes (8.6 per cent)

Identification

Next we would like to ask you a few questions about the ways in which incompetent teachers are identified in your district.

3   What are the various ways in which your district identifies incompetent teachers? [circle all numbers which apply]

    1   Complaints from parents or students (78 per cent, Yes)
    2   Student test results (46 per cent, Yes)
    3   Supervisor ratings (100 per cent, Yes)
    4   Student ratings (15.6 per cent, Yes)
    5   Complaints from other teachers (53.2 per cent, Yes)
    6   Other [Please specify] (7.1 per cent)

4   In some districts, schools (elementary, intermediate, or high school) conduct follow-up surveys of former students. These surveys are used to identify poorly performing teachers, as well as weaknesses in the instructional program. Is this practice ever used within your district? [circle number]

    1   No and we are unlikely to use this practice (53.9 per cent)
    2   No but we may use this practice in the future (19.2 per cent)
    3   Yes (26.9 per cent)

5   Some districts conduct exit interviews with parents when they move out of the district. A major purpose of these exit interviews is to identify teachers who may be performing poorly in the classroom. Does your district conduct exit interviews with parents to identify potentially unsatisfactory teachers? [circle number]

    1   No and we are unlikely to use this practice (78.0 per cent)
    2   No but we may use this practice in the future (17.7 per cent)
    3   Yes (4.3 per cent)

Remediation

Once a teacher is identified who is having difficulties in the classroom, some districts place the teacher in a formal remediation or assistance program. Placement in this program is a clear sign that the teacher's performance is unsatisfactory.

6 Has your district adopted a formal remediation program that is used to assist teachers who are judged to be unsatisfactory? [circle number]

   1 No and we are unlikely to use this practice (12.1 per cent)
   2 No but we may use this practice in the future (44.7 per cent)
   3 Yes (43.2 per cent)

Sanctions

If a teacher fails to improve his/her performance after being provided with assistance, districts generally use one or more of the following sanctions. We are interested in knowing which sanctions your district has used in recent years.

7 Have any of your *tenured* teachers received a 90-day notice for incompetence since 1 September 1982? [circle number]

   1 No (60.3 per cent)
   2 Yes (39.7 per cent)
   If Yes, how many teachers have received such notices? [Supply number] .... ($\bar{x}$ = 26 per 10,000; SD = 82)

8 Since 1 September 1982, have any of your teachers been involved in a hearing conducted by a Commission on Professional Competence? [circle number]

   1 No (90.1 per cent)
   2 Yes (9.9 per cent)
   If Yes, how many have been involved in a hearing

conducted by a Commission on Professional Competence?

[Supply number] .... ($\bar{x}$ = 2 per 10,000; SD = 18)

9 Since 1 September 1982 have any of your *probationary* teachers been notified that they would not be rehired for the succeeding year because of incompetence? [circle number]

1 No (79.4 per cent)
2 Yes (20.6 per cent)
If Yes, how many probationary teachers were notified that they would not be rehired due to incompetence? [Supply number] .... ($\bar{x}$ = 13 per 10,000; SD = 47)

10 Since 1 September 1982 have any of your *temporary* teachers been notified that they would not be rehired for the succeeding year because of unsatisfactory performance in the classroom? [circle number]

1 No (51.1 per cent)
2 Yes (48.9 per cent)
If Yes, how many temporary teachers were notified that they would not be rehired? [Supply number] .... ($\bar{x}$ = 29 per 10,000; SD = 54)

Reassignment

If a teacher fails to improve after receiving assistance, some districts find another assignment for the teacher.

11 Does your district ever remove teachers from the classroom because of incompetence and re-assign them to home-teaching duties (one-on-one in the student's home)? [circle number]

1 No and we are unlikely to use this practice (76.6 per cent)

2 No but we may use this practice in the future (12.8 per cent)

3 Yes (10.7 per cent)

12 Does your district ever take teachers out of a regular classroom teaching assignment because of incompetence and subsequently use them only as substitute teachers?

1 No and we are unlikely to use this practice (62.9 per cent)

2 No but we may use this practice in the future (17.9 per cent)

3 Yes (19.2 per cent)

13 Does your district ever transfer incompetent teachers to another school in hopes that they will be able to succeed in the new location? [circle number]

1 No (30.5 per cent)

2 Yes (69.5 per cent)

Resignations and Early Retirements

Each year there are teachers who resign or opt for early retirement. Some of these resignations and early retirements involve incompetent teachers who are induced by the administration to resign or to request early retirement. Oftentimes, these teachers decide to resign or to retire early because they are counseled out or because they want to avoid possible dismissal.

14 Since 1 September 1982 have any incompetent teachers resigned or taken early retirement because they were counseled out or wanted to avoid possible dismissal? [circle number]

1 No (32.6 per cent)

2 Yes (67.4 per cent)
   If Yes, how many such resignations or early retirements were there?
   [Supply number] . . . . ($\bar{x}$ = 78 per 10,000; SD = 142)

15　Some districts provide a variety of inducements to incompetent teachers for their resignations or early retirements. Which of the following inducements has your district provided to incompetent teachers in connection with their resignations or early retirements? [circle all letters which apply]

(a)　Employment as a consultant for a fixed period of time (36.9 per cent)

(b)　Outplacement counseling (professional assistance in preparing resumes, creating job search plans, and/or preparing for interviews) (4.3 per cent)

(c)　Cash settlement (lump sum payment) (27 per cent)

(d)　Medical coverage at district expense for a fixed period of time (46 per cent)

(e)　Employment as a substitute teacher (21.3 per cent)

(f)　Favorable recommendations for non-teaching positions (10.6 per cent)

(g)　Employment as a 'classified' employee for a fixed period of time (2.1 per cent)

(h)　Training at district expense to pursue another career (.7 per cent)

(i)　Paid leave for part of the school year (19.9 per cent)

(j)　A supplement to the state pension (7.8 per cent)

(k)　Life insurance paid by the district (policy has a cash reserve in addition to a death benefit) (2.8 per cent)

(l)　Removal of negative information from the personnel file (12.8 per cent)

(m)　Other [please specify] (4.5 per cent)

Background Information

We are also interested in having information about your district to help us interpret the data you have provided.

16　How many full-time equivalent teachers (including special education) are employed in your district?
[Supply number] .... ($\bar{x} = 287$; SD $= 338$)

17　Since 1 September 1979 has your district experienced declining enrollments? [Circle number]

1 No (52.5 per cent)
2 Yes (47.5 per cent) Declining enrollments: ($\bar{x}$ = 7; SD = 8)
   If Yes, please answer both of the following questions:
   (a) What was your *highest* student enrollment during the five-year period? [Supply number] ....
   (b) What was your *lowest* student enrollment during this five-year period? [Supply number] ....

18 What percentage of your full-time teachers are at the top of the salary schedule?
    [Supply number] .... ($\bar{x}$ = 43; SD = 23)
If you use any practices to deal with incompetent teachers that have not been mentioned in this questionnaire, please describe these practices on this page.

Your contribution to this effort is greatly appreciated. If you want a summary of the results, please write 'Copy of Results Requested' on the back of the return envelope and print your name and address below it. Thank you.

4 Hypotheses

In Chapter 2 we argued that the willingness of school administrators to confront incompetent teachers is influenced in part by four factors: (a) declining enrollments; (b) district size; (c) financial pressures; and (d) importance attached to teacher evaluation. One of the ways in which administrators confront incompetent teachers is to induce a resignation or an early retirement. Accordingly we stated and tested the following hypotheses:

H1: The more a district's enrollment declines, the higher its rate of induced exits.
H2: The smaller a district is in size, the higher its rate of induced exits.
H3: The more a district experiences financial pressure, the higher its rate of induced exits.
H4: The greater the importance attached to teacher evaluation by a district, the higher its rate of induced exits.

5 Variables

The five variables which were used to test the four hypotheses were measured as follows:

V1: Enrollment declines. If the district indicated that it had not experienced declining enrollments since 1 September 1979 the score was recorded as zero. If the district indicated that it had experienced declining enrollment in this time period, the magnitude of the enrollment decline was determined by dividing the lowest student enrollment during the five year period by the highest student enrollment and subtracting the answer from 1.00. The theoretical range of this measure is 0 to 1; the higher the value, the greater the level of enrollment decline.

Formula: $1.00 - (Q\# 17b\ /\ Q\# 17a) = V1$

V2: District size. Size of district was measured by using the number of full-time equivalent teachers employed in the district (obtained from answer to question number 16).

V3: Financial pressure. Since 55 to 70 per cent of a school district's budget goes for teacher salaries, we reasoned that districts with a large proportion of their teachers at the top of the salary range schedule would be under greater financial pressure than districts with a lower proportion of their teachers at this level. The proxy measure for financial pressure was the percentage of full-time teachers who were at the top of the district's salary schedule (obtained from question number 18 in the questionnaire.)

V4: Importance attached to teacher evaluation. The number of 90-day notices was used as a proxy measure for the importance attached to teacher evaluation. Issuing a 90-day notice is an extremely difficult and painful undertaking for most administrators, and it is a major indicator of their commitment to implementing a strong program in teacher evaluation. To standardize the rate across districts, the number of 90-day rates issued by the district was divided by the number of full-time equivalent teachers; the answer then was multiplied by 10,000.

Formula: $(Q\#7\ /\ Q\#16) \times 10,000 = V4$

V5: Induced exits. The rate of induced exits was calculated by dividing the number of incompetent teachers who had been induced to resign or to retire early by the total number of full-time equivalent teachers; the answer was multiplied by 10,000 to standardize the rate across districts.

Formula: $(Q\#14\ /\ Q\#16) \times 10,000 = V5$

6 Mode of Analysis

We used stepwise multiple regression analysis to test the four hypotheses.

7 Results

Each of the hypotheses was supported; moreover, the four variables accounted for 50.8 per cent (49.3 per cent, adjusted for degrees of freedom) of the variation in the induced exits reported by the districts. The results of the analyses are reported in tables 5 and 6.

Table 5: Zero order correlations among the five variables

Variable	Declining Enrollments	Pressure	Size	Exits
Financial pressures (percentage of teachers at top of salary schedule)	.395*			
Size of district	.007	.174		
Induced exits	.40*	.232*	−.235*	
Importance attached to teacher evaluation (90-day notices)	.143	.036	−.111	.602*

* p < .05
(n = 135; six cases contained missing values)

Table 6: Regression results for induced exits

Independent Variable	Coefficient	Stand. Dev. of Coefficient	T-Ratio
Importance attached to teacher evaluation (90-day notices)	0.92610	0.10830	8.55*
Declining enrollments	0.38956	0.09726	4.01*
Size of district	−0.08743	0.02763	−3.16*
Financial pressures (percentage of teachers at top of salary schedule)	0.85420	0.41470	2.06*

Multiple R = .713
Multiple R adjusted for degrees of freedom = .702
(n = 135; 6 cases contained missing values)
* p<.05

Appendix C: Case Study

1   Purpose

In the course of conducting a telephone survey of principals, Groves (1985) uncovered a school district with a relatively high rate of induced resignations and early retirements. We undertook a study of this district to understand the circumstances surrounding these induced exits. This particular district vividly illustrates how the conditions discussed in chapter 2 affect the responses of administrators to incompetent teachers.

2   Data Sources

In an effort to understand the dynamics of the induced exits in Ocean View (fictitious name), we relied on two major types of data: (a) published and unpublished documents and (b) interviews.

Documents

The description and analysis of what happened in Ocean View are based in part on the following documents: the collective bargaining agreement with teachers, the written guidelines of principals regarding teacher evaluation, district budgetary reports, enrollment reports, annual evaluations of unsatisfactory teachers, and principal classroom observation reports on unsatisfactory teachers.

Interview

Interviews were held with the following people: the Superintendent, the Board President, the middle school Principal, the two elementary principals, and a teacher who has been active in the local teachers' union. Through these interviews, we sought to ascertain information about each of the following topics:

(a) the ways in which the Superintendent and Board of Education manifest their commitment to evaluating and improving instruction;

(b) the changes which may have occurred in evaluating teachers and the reasons for these changes;

(c) the reactions to and impact of these changes;

(d) the criteria which are used to evaluate teachers;

(e) the procedures which are used to determine whether teachers satisfy the criteria;

(f) the nature of the remedial assistance which is provided to unsatisfactory teachers;

(g) the types of resources provided to principals in fulfilling their responsibilities for evaluating and improving instructional performance;

(h) the ways in which principals are held accountable for upgrading instructional performance;

(i) the types of sanctions which are used with unsatisfactory teachers;

(j) the types of inducements and assistance which are used in persuading incompetent teachers to leave the district; and

(k) the role of the union in the evaluation process.

References

ALEAMONI, L.M. 'Student ratings of instruction' in *Handbook of Teacher Evaluation*, pp. 110–145, edited by J. MILLMAN, Beverly Hills, California: SAGE Publications, Inc., 1981.

ANDERSON, H. 'A study of certain criteria of teaching effectiveness', *Journal of Experimental Education* 23 (September 1954): 41–71.

BAUM, J. and YOUNGBLOOD, S. 'Impact of an organizational control policy on absenteeism, performance, and satisfaction', *Journal of Applied Psychology* 60 (1975): 688–794.

BELL, D. 'Twelve modes of prediction — a preliminary sorting of approaches in the social sciences', *Daedalus* XCIII (1964): 45–73.

BLAU, P, *Bureaucracy in Modern Society*, New York: Random House, 1956.

BRAMMER, L. and HUMBERGER, F. *Outplacement and Inplacement Counseling*, Englewood Cliffs, New Jersey: Prentice-Hall Inc., 1984.

BRIDGES, E. 'Managing the incompetent teacher — What can principals do?' *NASSP Bulletin* 69 (February 1985): 57–65.

BRIDGES, E.M. with the assistance of Groves, B. *Managing the Incompetent Teacher*, Eugene, Oregon: ERIC Clearinghouse on Educational Management and Institute for Research on Educational Finance and Governance, Stanford University, 1990.

BRIDGES, E.M., and GUMPORT, P. 'The dismissal of tenured teachers for incompetence', Stanford, California: Institute for Research on Educational Finance and Governance, 1984. Technical Report.

BROOKOVER, W. 'Person-person interaction between teachers and pupils and teaching effectiveness', *Journal of Educational Research* 34 (December 1940): 272–87.

BRYAN, R.C. 'Reactions to teachers by students, parents and administrators', Kalamazoo, Michigan: Western Michigan University, 1963. Cooperative Research Project, No. 668.

BUELLESFIELD, H. 'Causes of failure among teachers', *Educational Administration and Supervision* 1 (September 1915): 439–45.

BURGER, W. 'A sick profession?' *Tulsa Law Journal* 5 (January 1968): 1–12.

CALIFORNIA COALITION FOR FAIR SCHOOL FINANCE, *Teaching in California: Rules and Procedures*, Menlo Park, California: The California Coalition for Fair School Finance, 1984.

CAREY, W.C. *Documenting Teacher Dismissal*, Salem, Oregon: Options Press, 1981.

CHAIT, R. and FORD, A. *Beyond Traditional Tenure*, San Francisco: Jossey-Bass Publishers, 1982.

CLAY, K., HUGHES, K., SEELY, J. and THAYER, A. *Public School Foundations: Their Organization and Operation*, Arlington, Virginia: Educational Research Service, Inc., 1985.

COHEN, P. 'Effectiveness of student-rating feedback for improving college instruction', *Research in Higher Education* 13 (1980): 321–41.

COHEN, P. 'Student ratings of instruction and achievement', *Review of Educational Research* 51 (Fall 1981): 281–309.

DARLING-HAMMOND, L. *Beyond the Commission Reports: The Coming Crisis in Teaching*, Santa Monica, California: Rand Corporation, 1984.

DICKMAN, F. and EMENER, W. 'Employee assistance programs: Basic concepts, attributes and an evaluation', *Personnel Administrator* 27 (August 1982): 55–62.

Digest of Education Statistics, 1990, Washington, D.C.: National Center for Education Statistics, 1990.

DIGILIO, A. 'When tenure is tyranny', *The Washington Post Education Review*, 12 August 1984, pp. 1, 12–14.

DILLMAN, D. *Mail and Telephone Surveys: The Total Design Method*, New York: John Wiley and Sons, Inc., 1978.

DOLGIN, A.B. 'Two types of due process: The role of supervision in teacher dismissal cases', *NASSP Bulletin* 65 (February 1981): 16–21.

EGBERT, L., BATTIT, G., WELCH, C. and BARTLETT, M. 'Reduction of postoperative pain by encouragement and instruction of patients', *New England Journal of Medicine*, 270 (1964): 825–27.

ELAM, S.M. *A Decade of Gallup Polls of Attitudes Toward Education 1969–1978*, Bloomington, Indiana: Phi Delta Kappa, 1978.

ELMORE, R. and McLAUGHLIN, M. *Reform and Retrenchment: The Politics of California School Finance Reform*, Cambridge: Ballinger Publishing Company, 1982.

EVANS, D. 'Reflections of a Principal on the Procedures for the Dismissal of a Permanent Teacher.' Mimeographed (no date).

FEISTRITZER, C. *The Condition of Teaching*, Princeton, New Jersey: Princeton University Press, 1983.

FINER, J. 'Ineffective assistance of counsel', *Cornell Law Review* 58 (July 1973): 1077–120.

FINLAYSON, H.J. 'Incompetence and teacher dismissal', *Phi Delta Kappan* 61 (September 1979): 69.

FORD, R.C. and McLAUGHLIN, F.S. 'Employee assistance programs: A descriptive survey of ASPA members', *Personnel Administrator* 26 (September 1981): 29–35.

FOURNIER, G. 'A study of the experiences of Tennessee public secondary school principals in teacher dismissals', Ed.D. dissertation, George Peabody College for Teachers, Vanderbilt University, 1984.

FRELS, K. and COOPER, T.T. *A Documentation System for Teacher Improvement or Termination*, Topeka, Kansas: National Organization on Legal Problems of Education, 1982.

GAGE, N., RUNKEL, P. and CHATTERJEE, B. 'Equilibrium theory and behavior change: An experiment in feedback from pupils to teachers', Champaign, Illinois: Bureau of Educational Research, College of Education, University of Illinois, 1960.

GARDNER, S. *Status of the American Public School Teacher 1980–81*, Washington, D.C.: National Education Association, 1982.

GHISELLI, E. 'The validity of aptitude tests in personnel selection', *Personnel Psychology*, 26 (1973): 461–477.

GOFFMAN, E. 'On face-work', *Psychiatry* 18 (1955), pp. 213–31.

GOLD, C., DENNIS, R. and GRAHAM, J. 'Reinstatement after termination: Public school teachers', *Industrial and Labor Relations Review* 31 (April 1978): 310–21.

GOODE, W. 'The protection of the inept', *American Sociological Review* 32 (February 1967): 5–19.

GRACE, G. 'Headteachers' judgments of teacher competence: Principles and procedures in ten inner-city schools' in *Selection, Certification and Control*, pp. 103–126, edited by P. Broadfoot. Lewes: Falmer Press, 1984.

GRANT, W. and SNYDER, T. *Digest of Education Statistics 1983–84*, Washington, D.C.: National Center for Education Statistics, 1984.

GROSS, J. *Teachers on Trial*. Ithaca, N.Y.: Industrial Labor Relations Press, 1988.

GROVE, A. *High Output Management*, New York: Vintage Press, 1985.

GROVES, B. 'An organizational approach to teacher evaluation', Ed. D. dissertation, Stanford University, 1985.

GUTHRIE, H. and WILLOWER, D. 'The ceremonial congratulation: An analysis of principal observation reports of classroom teaching', *High School Journal* 56 (March 1973): 284–90.

HALLINGER, P. *Assessing the Instructional Management Behavior of Principals*. Unpublished Ed. D. dissertation, School of Education, Stanford University, 1983.

HARPER, W.P. and GAMMON, R.T. 'Defining inadequate performance under the North Carolina Tenured Teacher Fair Dismissal Act', *Campbell Law Review* 3 (1981): 77–102.

HEAVILIN, B.A. 'Confusion worse confounded: Incompetence among public school teachers', *Teacher Educator* 16 (Fall 1980): 11–20.

HEISNER, J.D. 'The ugly face of mediocrity!' *Instructor* 89 (March 1980): 18, 20.

HELLER, S. 'More colleges offering programs to help employees cope with personal problems', *Chronicle of Higher Education*, XXVIII, 12 (May 16, 1984), 21–3.

HERALD, E. 'Improving New York state public schools: Will proposals to license teachers eliminate incompetence?' *Buffalo Law Review* 29 (1980): 371–98.

HERSEY, P. and BLANCHARD, K. *Management of Organizational Behavior*, Englewood Cliffs, New Jersey: Prentice-Hall, Inc., 1982.

HOLMES, T. and MASUDA, M. 'Life change and illness susceptibility', in *Stressful Life Events*, pp. 45–72, edited by B.S. DOHRENWEND and B.P. DOHRENWEND, New York: John Wiley and Sons, Inc., 1974.

HOSOKAWA, E. and THORESON, R. *Employee Assistance Programs in Higher Education: Alcohol, Mental Health, and Professional Development Program-*

ming for Faculty and Staff, Springfield, Illinois: Charles C. Thomas, Publisher, 1984.

HUNTER, M. and RUSSELL, D. 'How can I plan more effective lessons?' *Instructor* 87 (September 1977): 74–5+.

JANIS, I.L. and MANN, L. *Decision Making*, New York: The Free Press, 1977.

JENTZ, B. *Entry: The Hiring, Start-Up, and Supervision of Administrators*, New York: McGraw-Hill, 1982.

JOHNSON, J. and LEVENTHAL, H. 'Effects of accurate expectations and behavioral instructions on reactions during a noxious medical examination', *Journal of Personality and Social Psychology* 29 (1974): 710–8.

JOHNSON, S.M. 'Performance-based staff layoffs in the public schools: Implementation and outcomes', *Harvard Educational Review* 50 (May 1980): 214–33.

JOHNSON, S. *Teacher Unions in Schools*, Philadelphia, Pennsylvania: Temple University Press, 1984.

JONES, D. *Arbitration and Industrial Discipline*, Ann Arbor, Michigan: Bureau of Industrial Relations, The University of Michigan, 1961.

JONES, R. 'The prediction of teaching efficiency from objective measures', *Journal of Experimental Education* 15 (1946): 85–99.

KAUFMAN, H. *Professionals in Search of Work: Coping with the Stress of Job Loss and Unemployment*, New York: Wiley, 1982.

KELLEHER, P. 'Inducing incompetent teachers to resign', *Phi Delta Kappan* 66 (January 1985): 362–64.

KERR, D.H. 'Teaching competence and teacher education in the United States', in *Handbook of Teaching and Policy*, pp. 126–49, edited by L. SHULMAN and G. SYKES, New York: Longman, 1983.

KING, J. *The Law of Medical Malpractice*, St. Paul, Minnesota: West Publishing Company, 1977.

KUTNER, S. 'The effect of pension wealth on the age of retirement', Project Report No. 84–A9, Stanford University, Stanford, California: Institute for Research on Educational Finance and Governance, 1984.

LARSON, D.H. 'Advice for the principal: Dealing with unsatisfactory teacher performance', *NASSP Bulletin* 65 (February 1981): 10–11.

LATHAM, G.P. and WEXLEY, K. N. *Increasing Productivity Through Performance Appraisal*, Reading, Massachusetts: Ballinger Publishing Company, 1981.

LEBEIS, B. 'Teachers' tenure legislation', *Michigan Law Review* 37 (1939): 430–40.

LEISTER, B.M. 'Incompetent teachers and misguided courts', *Phi Kappa Phi Journal* 61 (Spring 1981): 47–8.

LEVINSON, H. *Emotional Health in the World of Work*, New York: Harper and Row, 1964.

LEVY, J. and McGEE, K. 'Childbirth as crisis: A test of Janis' theory of communication and stress resolution', *Journal of Personality and Social Psychology* 31 (1975): 171–9.

LINS, L. 'The prediction of teaching efficiency', *Journal of Experimental Education* 15 (1946): 2–60.

LITTLER, S. 'Why teachers fail', *Home and School Education* 33 (March 1914): 255–56.

Edwin M. Bridges

LORTIE, D. *The Schoolteacher: A Sociological Study*, Chicago: The University of Chicago Press, 1975.

McCALL, W. and KRAUSE, G. 'Measurement of teacher merit', *Journal of Educational Research* 53 (October 1959): 73–5.

McDANIEL, S.H. and McDANIEL, T.R. 'How to weed out incompetent teachers without getting hauled into court', *Nat'l Elem Prin* 59 (March 1980): 31–6.

McDERMOTT, T.J. and NEWHAMS, T.H. 'Discharge — reinstatement: What happens thereafter', *Industrial and Labor Relations Review* 24 (July 1971): 526–40.

McGREAL, T. *Successful Teacher Evaluation*, Alexandria, Virginia: Association for Supervision and Curriculum Development, 1983.

McLAUGHLIN, M. and PFEIFER, R. *Teacher Evaluation: Improvement, Accountability, and Effective Learning*, New York: Teachers College Press, 1988.

McLAUGHLIN, M., PFEIFER, R., SWANSON-OWENS, D. and YEE, S. 'Why teachers won't teach', *Phi Delta Kappan*, 67 (February 1986): 420–426.

MADSEN, I. 'The prediction of teaching success', *Educational Administration and Supervision* 13 (January 1927): 39–47.

MALINOWSKI, A.A. 'An empirical analysis of discharge cases and the work history of employees reinstated by Labor arbitratiors', *The Arbitration Journal* 36 (March 1981): 31–46.

MARGERISON, C. *Managerial Problem Solving*, London: McGraw-Hill, 1974.

MARKS, F. and CATHCART, A. 'Discipline within the legal profession: Is it self-regulation?' *U of Ill Law Forum (1974)*: 193–236.

MARGOLESE, A. 'Dismissal for cause', *California School Boards* 41 (October-November 1982): 8–11.

MEDLEY, D., COKER, H. and SOAR, R. *Measurement-Based Evaluation of Teacher Performance*, New York: Longman Inc., 1984.

MITCHELL, T.R., GREEN, S.G. and WOOD, R.E. 'An attributional model of leadership and the poor performing subordinate: Development and validation', *Research in Organizational Behavior* 3 (1981): 197–234.

MUNNELLY, R.J. 'Dealing with teacher incompetence: Supervision and evaluation in a due process framework', *Contemporary Education* 50 (Summer 1979): 221–5.

MUNNELLY, R.J. 'Dismissal for professional incompetence', *Education Digest* 50 (November 1979): 10–13.

MURNANE, R.J. 'Understanding the sources of teaching competence: Choices, skills, and the limits of training', *Teacher's College Record* 84 (Spring 1983): 564–9.

MURNANE, R. 'Selection and survival in the teacher labor market', *The Review of Economics and Statistics* 66 (August 1984): 513–8.

NATIONAL EDUCATION ASSOCIATION. 'The problem of tenure', *NEA Research Bulletin*, 2 (1924): 143–145.

NATRIELLO, G. 'Teachers' perceptions of the frequency of evaluation and assessments of their effort and effectiveness', *American Educational Research Journal* 21 (Fall 1984): 579–95.

NEILL, S.B., and CUSTIS, J. *Staff Dismissal: Problems and Solutions*, Arlington, Virginia: American Association of School Administrators, 1978.

O'REILLY, C.A. and WETTZ, B.A. 'Managing marginal employees: The use of warnings and dismissals', *Administrative Science Quarterly* 25 (1980): 467–84.

OZSOGOMONYAN, N. 'Teacher dismissals under section 13447 of the California education code', *Hastings Law Journal* 27 (July 1976): 1401–29.

PALKER, P. 'How to deal with incompetent teachers', *Teacher* 97 (January 1980): 42–5.

PECK, M. *The Road Less Traveled*, New York: Simon and Schuster, 1978.

PELLICER, L.O. and HENDRIX, O.B. 'A practical approach to remediation and dismissal', *NASSP Bulletin* 64 (March 1980): 57–62.

PETERSON, K. 'The principal's tasks', *Administrator's Notebook*, 26 (1977–78): 1–4.

PHAY, R.E. *Legal Issues in Public School Administrative Hearings*, Topeka, Kansas: NOLPE, 1982.

PLISKO, V. *The Condition of Education*, Washington, D.C.: Superintendent of Documents, U.S. Government Printing Office, 1983.

RABIN, R. 'The duty of fair representation in arbitration', in *The Duty of Fair Representation*, pp. 84–96, edited by J. MCKELVEY. Ithaca, N.Y.: New York School of Industrial and Labor Relations, Cornell University, 1977.

REILLY, R.R. and CHAO, G.T. 'Validity and fairness of some alternative employee selection procedures', *Personnel Psychology*, 35 (1982): 1–62.

REMERS, H. 'Reliability and "Halo" effect of high school and college students' judgments of their teachers', *Journal of Applied Psychology* 18 (October 1939): 619–30.

RONEY, R.K. and PERRY, I.O. 'Where the buck stops: Tenure laws and incompetency', *NASSP Bulletin* 61 (February 1977): 45–50.

ROSENBERGER, D.S. and PLIMPTON, R.A. 'Teacher incompetence and the courts', *Journal of Law and Education* 4 (July 1975): 468–86.

ROSENSHINE, B. 'The stability of teacher effects upon student achievement', in *The Appraisal of Teaching*, pp. 341–50, edited by G. BORICH. Reading, Massachusetts: Addison-Wesley Publishing Company, 1977.

SCHLECTY, P. and VANCE, V. 'Do academically able teachers leave education? The North Carolina case', *Phi Delta Kappan* 63 (1981): 106–12.

SCHMITT, F.E. and WOOLRIDGE, P.J. 'Psychological preparation of surgical patients', *Nursing Research* 22 (1973): 108–16.

SCHMITT, N., GOODING, R., NOE, R. and KIRSCH, M. 'Meta-analyses of validity studies published between 1964 and the investigation of study characteristics', *Personnel Psychology*, 37 (1984): 407–422.

SCHNIEDER, B. *Staffing Organizations*, Santa Monica, California. Goodyear Publishing Company, Inc., 1976.

'School maze: Teacher dismissal and layoff in California', *Cal-Tax Research Bulletin* 56 (November 1981): 1–8.

SCOTT, C. *Indefinite Teacher Tenure*, New York City: Bureau of Publications, Teachers College, Columbia University, 1934.

SCRIVEN, M. 'Duty-based teacher evaluation', *Journal of Personnel Evaluation in Education*, 1, (July 1988): 319–334.

SHAFER, P. 'Teacher Dismissals', Presentation at 5th Annual Buros-Nebraska Symposium on Measurement and Testing, Lincoln, Nebraska, October 2, 1987.

SIMON, D. 'Personal reasons for the dismissal of teachers in smaller schools', *Journal of Educational Research* 29 (April 1936): 585–8.

SPROULL, L. 'Managing educational programs', *Human Organization* 40 (1981): 113–22.

STALNECKER, J. and REMERS, H. 'Can students discriminate traits associated with success in teaching?' *Journal of Applied Psychology* 12 (December 1929): 605ff.

STEINMETZ, L. *Managing the Marginal and Unsatisfactory Performer*, Reading, Massachusetts: Addison-Wesley Publishing Company, 1969.

STELZER, L. and BANTHIN, J. *Teachers Have Rights, Too*, Boulder, Colorado: ERIC Clearinghouse for Social Studies/Social Science Education, 1980.

STOEBERL, P. and SCHNIEDERJANS, M. 'The ineffective subordinate: A management survey', *Personnel Administrator* 26 (February 1981): 72–6.

SUMMERS, C. 'The individual employee's right under the collective agreement: What constitutes fair representation?' in *The Duty of Fair Representation*, pp. 60–83, edited by J. McKELVEY. Ithaca, N.Y.: New York School of Industrial and Labor Relations, Cornell University, 1977.

SZABO, M. *Crucible or Cradle; Variations in Working Conditions and the Socialization of New Teachers*. Unpublished doctoral dissertation, Stanford University, Stanford, California, 1990.

TAYLOR, H., and RUSSELL, J. 'The relationship of validity coefficients to the practical effectiveness of tests in selection: Discussion and tables', *Journal of Applied Psychology* 23 (October 1939): 565–78.

THURSTON, P.W. 'Tenured teacher dismissal in Illinois, 1975–1979', *Illinois Bar Journal* 69 (March 1981): 422–31.

TIGGES, J. 'What constitutes "Incompetency" or "Inefficiency" as a ground for dismissal or demotion of public school teacher', 4 (1965) *ALR* 3d: 1090–120.

TRASK, A. 'Principals, teachers, and supervision: Dilemmas and solutions', *Administrator's Notebook* XIII (December 1964): 1–4.

TUCKMAN, B. and OLIVER, W. 'Effectiveness of feedback to teachers as a function of source', *Journal of Educational Psychology* 59 (1968): 297–301.

VOGEL, J. and DELGADO, R. 'To tell the truth: Physicians' duty to disclose medical mistakes', *UCLA Law Review* 28 (October 1980): 52–94.

WANOUS, J. 'Effects of a realistic job preview on job acceptance, job attitudes, and job survival', *Journal of Applied Psychology* 58 (1973): 327–32.

WARD, B.A. 'Beyond test scores as indicators of teacher incompetence', *California Journal of Teacher Education* 9 (Summer 1982): 24–41.

WILLIAMS, D., HOWARD, L., McDONALD, D. and RENEE, M. 'Why teachers fail', *Newsweek*, 13 (September 24, 1984): 64–70.

WISE, A., DARLING-HAMMOND, L., McLAUGHLIN, M. and BERNSTEIN, H. *Case Studies for Teacher Evaluation: A Study of Effective Practices*, Santa Monica, California: Rand Corporation, 1984.

ZIRKEL, P. and BARGERSTOCK, C. *The Law on Reduction-in-Force*, Arlington, Virginia: Educational Research Service, Inc., 1980.

Index